THE EDGE OF THE
UNKNOWN

THE EDGE OF THE
UNKNOWN

SIR ARTHUR
CONAN DOYLE

BARNES
&NOBLE
BOOKS
NEW YORK

This edition published by Marboro Books Corp.,
a division of Barnes & Noble, Inc.

1992 Barnes & Noble Books

ISBN 0-88029-986-X

Printed and bound in the United States of America

M 9 8 7 6 5 4 3 2 1

CONTENTS

I	THE RIDDLE OF HOUDINI	11
II	THE SHADOWS ON THE SCREEN	49
III	NOTES FROM A STRANGE MAIL-BAG	63
IV	THE GHOST OF THE MOAT	77
V	THE LAW OF THE GHOST	81
VI	ALLEGED POSTHUMOUS WRITINGS OF KNOWN AUTHORS	95
VII	SOME CURIOUS PERSONAL EXPERIENCES	111
VIII	DWELLERS ON THE BORDER	119
IX	A STRANGE PROPHET	133
X	A LONDON GHOST	145
XI	THE HALF-WAY HOUSE OF MATTER	151
XII	A REMARKABLE MAN	163
XIII	THE RIFT IN THE VEIL	177
XIV	A NEW LIGHT ON OLD CRIMES	191
XV	SINGULAR RECORDS OF A CIRCLE	209

PREFACE

There is a passage in that charming book "The Bridge of San Luis Rey" which runs as follows: "She was one of these persons who have allowed their lives to be gnawed away because they have fallen in love with an idea several centuries before its appointed appearance in the history of Civilization. She hurled herself against the obstinacy of her time." We who believe in the psychic revelation, and who appreciate that a perception of these things is of the utmost importance, certainly have hurled ourselves against the obstinacy of our time. Possibly we have allowed some of our lives to be gnawed away in what, for the moment, seemed a vain and thankless quest. Only the future can show whether the sacrifice was worth it. Personally I think that it was. Among the various chords which are struck in this little book there may be some to which the mind of the reader will respond, and which may entice him also in the search for the Holy Grail.

ARTHUR CONAN DOYLE.

Crowborough.
1930.

THE EDGE OF THE
UNKNOWN

I

THE RIDDLE OF HOUDINI

WHO WAS the greatest medium-baiter of modern times? Undoubtedly Houdini. Who was the greatest physical medium of modern times? There are some who would be inclined to give the same answer. I do not see how it can ever now be finally and definitely proved, but circumstantial evidence may be very strong, as Thoreau said when he found a trout in the milk jug. I foresee that the subject will be debated for many years to come, so perhaps my opinion, since I knew him well, and always entertained this possibility in my mind, may be of interest. If others add their experience in order to support or disprove my own surmises, then some result may eventually be obtained.

I will first give some of my own personal impressions of Houdini. I will then dwell on some phases of his career which show his singular character, and I will then endeavour to give the argument as to the source of his unique powers.

Let me say, in the first instance, that in a long life which has touched every side of humanity, Houdini is far and away the most curious and intriguing character whom I have ever encountered. I have met better men, and I have certainly met very many worse ones, but I have never met a man who had such strange contrasts in his nature, and whose actions and motives it was more difficult to foresee or to reconcile.

I will first, as is only proper, dwell upon the great good which lay in his nature. He had the essential masculine quality of courage to a supreme degree. Nobody has ever done, and nobody in all human probability will ever do, such reckless feats of daring. His whole life was one long succession of them, and when I say that amongst them was the leaping from one aeroplane to another, with handcuffed hands at the height of three thousand feet, one can form an idea of the extraordinary lengths that he would go. In this, however, as in much more that concerned him, there was a certain psychic element which he was ready to admit freely. He told me that a voice which was independent of his own reason or judgment told him what to do and how to do it. So long as he obeyed the voice he was assured of safety. "It all comes as easy as stepping off a log," said he to me, "but I have to wait for the voice. You stand there before a jump, swallowing the yellow stuff that every man has in him. Then at last you hear the voice and you jump. Once I jumped on my own and I nearly broke my neck." This was the nearest admission that I ever had from him that I was right in thinking that there was a psychic element which was essential to every one of his feats.

Apart from his amazing courage, he was remarkable for his cheery urbanity in every-day life. One could not wish a better companion so long as one was with him, though he might do and say the most unexpected things when one was absent. He was, like most Jews, estimable in his family relationships. His love for his dead mother seemed to be the ruling passion of his life, which he expressed on all sorts of public occasions in a way which was, I am sure, sincere, but is strange to our colder Western blood. There were many things in Houdini which were as Oriental as there were in our own Disraeli. He was devoted also to his wife, and with good reason, for she was as devoted to him, but again his intimacy showed itself in unconventional ways. When in his examination before the Senatorial Committee he was hard-pressed by some defender of Spiritualism who impugned his motives in his violent and vindictive campaign against mediums, his answer was to turn to his wife and to say, "I have always been a good boy, have I not?"

Another favourable side of his character was his charity. I have heard, and am quite prepared to believe, that he was the last refuge of the down-and-outer, especially if he belonged to his own profession of showman. This charity extended even beyond the grave, and if he heard of any old magician whose tombstone needed repair he took it upon himself at once to set the matter right. Willie Davenport in Australia, Bosco in Germany, and many others of his profession were the objects of these pious offices. Whatever he did was done upon a large scale. He had many pensioners whom he did not know by sight. One man embraced him in the street, and upon Houdini angrily demanding who the devil he was, he answered, "Why, I am the man whose rent you have paid for the last ten years." He was devoted to children, though he had none of his own. He was never too busy to give a special free performance for the youngsters. At Edinburgh he was so shocked at the bare feet of the kiddies that he had them all into the theatre, and fitted them then and there with five hundred pairs of boots. He was the greatest publicity agent that ever lived, so that it is not ill-natured to surmise that the local papers had been advised beforehand, and that the advertisement was well worth it. There were other occasions, however, when his charity was less ostentatious. Animals too were loved by him, and he had a peculiar talent for taming them and teaching them tricks. All these ingredients in one impulsive personality surely make up a very lovable man. It is true that his generosity was curiously mixed with frugality, so that even while he was giving away his earnings at a rate which alarmed his wife, he would put an indignant comment in his diary because he had been charged two shillings for the pressing of his clothes.

So much for his virtues—and most of us would be very glad to have as goodly a list. But all he did was extreme, and there was something to be placed in the other scale.

A prevailing feature of his character was a vanity which was so obvious and childish that it became more amusing than offensive. I can remember, for example, that when he introduced his brother to me, he did it by saying, "This is the brother of the great Houdini." This without any twinkle of humour and in a perfectly natural manner.

This enormous vanity was combined with a passion for publicity which knew no bounds, and which must at all costs be gratified. There was no consideration of any sort which would restrain him if he saw his way to an advertisement. Even when he laid flowers upon the graves of the dead it was in the prearranged presence of the local photographers.

It was this desire to play a constant public part which had a great deal to do with his furious campaign against Spiritualism. He knew that the public took a keen interest in the matter, and that there was unlimited publicity to be had from it. He perpetually offered large sums to any medium who would do this or that, knowing well that even in the unlikely event of the thing being done he could always raise some objection and get out of it. Sometimes his tactics were too obvious to be artistic. In Boston he arrived by prearrangement before a great crowd at the City Hall and walked solemnly up the steps with ten thousand dollars' worth of stock in his hand, which represented one of his perennial stakes against phenomena. This was in connection with his engagement on a tour of the music-halls. His favourite argument, and that of many of his fellow-conjurers, was this flourishing of dollar-wads. It is obviously absurd, since the money will only be paid if you satisfy the challenger, and since the challenger has to pay the money he naturally never will be satisfied. The classical instance is that of the *Scientific American* magazine, which offered a large sum for any well-attested psychic phenomenon, but on being confronted with the Crandon phenomena, which are perhaps the best attested in the whole annals of psychical research, found reasons for withholding the money. I remember that when I arrived in New York, Houdini offered some huge sum that he could do anything which I had ever seen a medium do. I at once accepted his challenge, and proposed as a test that he should materialize the face of my mother in such a way that others besides myself who had known her in life could recognize it. I heard no more of the matter after that, and yet in England a medium had actually done this. I would have brought my witnesses across the Atlantic had the test been accepted.

I am quite prepared to think that Houdini's campaign against mediums did temporary good so far as false mediums goes, but it was so indiscriminate and accompanied by so much which was intolerant and offensive that it turned away the sympathy and help which Spiritualists, who are anxious for the cleanliness of their own movement, would gladly have given him. The unmasking of false mediums is our urgent duty, but when we are told that, in spite of our own evidence and that of three generations of mankind, there are no real ones we lose interest, for we know that we are speaking to an ignorant man. At the same time, the States, and in a lesser degree our own people, do need stern supervision. I admit that I underrated the corruption in the States. What first brought it home to me was that my friend Mrs. Crandon told me that she had received price lists from some firm which manufactures fraudulent instruments for performing tricks. If such a firm can make a living, there must be some villainy about, and a more judicious Houdini might well find a useful field of activity. It is these hyenas who retard our progress. I have myself had a hand in exposing more than one of them.

There was a particular Hall in Boston which Houdini used for his tirades against the spirits. Some weeks after his campaign a curious and disagreeable phenomenon broke out there. Showers of gravel or of small pebbles fell continually among the audience, and several people suffered minor injuries. A police watch was kept up for some time, and eventually it was shown that a staid employee, whose record was an excellent one, was in the habit, without rhyme or reason, of stealing up to the gallery and throwing these missiles down into the stalls. When tried for the offense he could only say that a senseless but overpowering impulse caused him to do it. Many psychic students would be prepared to consider that the incident would bear the interpretation of a poltergeist on the one side and an obsession on the other.

There was another incident at Boston of a very much more serious kind, and one which bears out my assertion that where there was an advertisement to be gained Houdini was a dangerous man. The remarkable psychic powers of Mrs. Crandon, the famous "Margery," were at that time under examination by the committee of the *Scientific American*. Various members of this committee had sat many times with the Crandons, and some of them had been completely converted to the psychic explanation, while others, though unable to give any rational explanation of the phenomena, were in different stages of dissent. It would obviously be an enormous feather in Houdini's cap if he could appear on the scene and at once solve the mystery. What a glorious position to be in! Houdini laid his plans and was so sure of success that before going to Boston he wrote a letter, which I saw, to a mutual friend in London, announcing that he was about to expose her. He would have done it, too, had it not been for an interposition which was miraculous. I think well enough of Houdini to hope that he would have held his hand if he could have realized the ruin and disgrace which his success would have brought upon his victims. As it was, the thought of the tremendous advertisement swallowed up his scruples. All America was watching, and he could not resist the temptation.

He had become familiar in advance with the procedure of the Crandon circle, and with the types of phenomena. It was easy for him to lay his plans. What he failed to take into account was that the presiding spirit, Walter, the dead brother of Mrs. Crandon, was a very real and live entity, who was by no means inclined to allow his innocent sister to be made the laughing-stock of the continent. It was the unseen Walter who checkmated the carefully-laid plans of the magician.

The account of what occurred I take from the notes which were taken by the circle at the time. The first phenomenon to be tested was the ringing of an electric bell which could only be done by pressing down a flap of wood, well out of the reach of the medium. The room was darkened, but the bell did not ring. Suddenly the angry voice of Walter was heard.

"You have put something to stop the bell ringing, Houdini, you——" he cried.

Walter has a wealth of strong language and makes no pretence at all to be a very elevated being. They all have their use over there. On this occasion, at least, the use was evident, for when the light was turned up, there was the rubber from the end of a pencil stuck into the angle of the flap in such a way as to make it impossible that it could descend and press the bell. Of course, Houdini professed complete ignorance as to how it got there, but who else had the deft touch to do such a thing in the dark, and why was it only in his presence that such a thing occurred? It is clear that if he could say afterwards, when he had quietly removed the rubber, that his arrival had made all further trickery impossible, he would have scored the first trick in the game.

He should have taken warning and realized that he was up against powers which were too strong for him, and which might prove dangerous if provoked too far. But the letters he had written and boasts he had made cut off his retreat. The second night landed him in a very much worse mess than the first one. He had brought with him an absurd box which was secured in front by no fewer than eight padlocks. One would have thought that it was a gorilla rather than a particularly gentle lady who was about to be confined within. The forces behind Margery showed what they thought of this contraption by bursting the whole front open the moment Margery was fastened into it. This very unexpected development Houdini endeavoured to explain away, but he found it difficult to give a reason why, if the box was so vulnerable, it was worth while to bring it with so much pomp and ceremony, with eight padlocks and many other gadgets, all the way from New York to Boston.

However, much worse was to come. The lady was put into the re-constituted box, her arms protruding through holes on each side. Houdini was observed without any apparent reason to pass his hand along the lady's arm, and so into the box. Presently, after some experiments, the lady's arms were placed inside and the attempt was to be made to ring the bell-box while only her head projected. Suddenly the terrible Walter intervened.

"Houdini, you—blackguard!" he thundered. "You have put a rule into the cabinet. You——! Remember, Houdini, you won't live for ever. Some day you've got to die."

The lights were turned on, and, shocking to relate, a two-foot folding rule was found lying in the box. It was a most deadly trick, for, of course, if the bell had rung Houdini would have demanded a search of the cabinet, the rule would have been found, it would, if held between the teeth, have enabled the medium to have reached and pressed down the flap of the bell-box, and all America would have resounded next day with the astuteness of Houdini and the proven villainy of the Crandons. I do not think that even the friends of the latter could have got over the patent facts. It was the most dangerous moment of their career, and only Walter saved them from ruin.

For the moment Houdini was completely overcome, and cowered, as well he might, before the wrath of the unseen. His offence was so obvious that no better excuse occurred to him, when he had rallied his senses, than that the rule had been left there by accident by some sub-ordinate. When one considers, however, that no other tool upon earth, neither a hammer, a chisel, nor a wrench, but only a folding two-foot rule, could have sustained the charge, one realizes how hopeless was his position. But one of Houdini's characteristics was that nothing in this world or the next could permanently abash him. He could not suggest that they were guilty considering that the Crandons had actually asked to have the cabinet examined after she had entered, and Houdini had refused. Yet, incredible as it may seem, he had his advertisement after all, for he flooded America with a pamphlet to say that he had shown that the Crandons were frauds, and that he had in some un-specified way exposed them. Since the cabinet had become a delicate subject his chief accusation was that Mrs. Crandon had in some way rung the bell-box by stretching out her foot. He must have known, though his complaisant audiences did not, that the bell-box was continually rung while some sitter was permitted to hold it in his hands, and even to rise and walk away with it.

Speaking with a full knowledge, I say that this Boston incident was never an exposure of Margery, but it was a very real exposure of Houdini, and is a most serious blot upon his career.

To account for the phenomena he was prepared to assert that not only the doctor, but that even members of the committee were in senseless collaboration with the medium. The amazing part of the business was that other members of the committee seemed to have been overawed by the masterful conjurer, and even changed their very capable secretary, Mr. Malcolm Bird, at his behest. Mr. Bird, it may be remarked, with a far better brain than Houdini, and with a record of some fifty séances, had by this time been entirely convinced of the truth of the phenomena.

It may seem unkind that I should dwell upon these matters now that Houdini has gone to his account, but what I am writing now I also published during his lifetime. I deal gently with the matter, but I have to remember that its importance far transcends any worldly consideration, and that the honour of the Crandons is still impugned in many minds by the false charges which were not only circulated in print, but were shouted by Houdini from the platforms of a score of music-halls with a violence which browbeat and overbore every protest from the friends of truth. Houdini did not yet realize the gravity of his own actions, or the consequences which they entailed. The Crandons are themselves the most patient and forgiving people in the world, treating the most irritating opposition with a good-humoured and amused tolerance. But there are other forces which are beyond human control, and from that day the shadow lay heavy upon Houdini. His anti-Spiritualist agitation became more and more unreasoning until it bordered upon a mania which could only be explained in some quarters by supposing that he was in the pay of certain clerical fanatics, an accusation which I do not believe. It is true that in order to preserve some show of reason he proclaimed that he wished only to attack dishonest mediums, but as in the same breath he would assert that there were no honest ones, his moderation was more apparent than real. If he had consulted the reports of the National Association of American Spiritualists he would have found that this representative body was far more efficient in exposing those swindlers than he had ever been, for they had the necessary experience by which the true can be separated from the false.

I suppose that at that time Houdini was, from an insurance point of view, so far as bodily health goes, the best life of his age in America. He was in constant training, and he used neither alcohol nor tobacco. Yet all over the land warnings of danger arose. He alluded in public to the matter again and again. In my own home circle I had the message some months before his death, "Houdini is doomed, doomed, doomed!" So seriously did I take this warning that I would have written to him had I the least hope that my words could have any effect. I knew, however, by previous experience, that he always published my letters, even the most private of them, and that it would only give him a fresh pretext for ridiculing that which I regard as a sacred cause.

But as the months passed and fresh warnings came from independent sources, both I and, as I believe, the Crandons became seriously alarmed for his safety. He was, on one side of his character, so fine a fellow that even those who were attacked in this monstrous way were unwilling that real harm should befall him.

But he continued to rave, and the shadow continued to thicken. I have an American friend who writes in the press under the name of Samri Frikell. He is really Fulton Oursler, the distinguished novelist, whose *Step-child of the Moon* is, in my judgment, one of the best of recent romances. Oursler was an intimate friend of Houdini, and he has allowed me to quote some of his experiences.

"You know him as well as I do," writes Oursler. "You knew the immense vanity of the man. You know that he loved to be important. My experience with him for the last three months of his life was most peculiar. He would call me on the telephone at seven o'clock in the morning and he would be in a quarrelsome mood. He would talk for an hour telling me how important he was and what a great career he was making. In his voice was a hysterical, almost feminine, note of rebellion, as if his hands were beating against an immutable destiny.

"In all these cases Houdini portrayed to me a clear sense of impending doom. This is not an impression which I have received subsequent to his death. But I commented upon it at the time. I believe that Houdini sensed the coming of his death, but did not know that it meant death. He didn't know what it meant, but he hated it and his soul screamed out in indignation."

Some time later he telephoned to the same friend in a way which showed that his surmise had become more definite. "I am marked for death," said he. "I mean that they are predicting my death in spirit circles all over the country." At that time he was starting in perfect health upon that tour of the Vaudevilles which was destined to be the last of his career. Within a few weeks he was dead.

The details of that death were in many ways most singular. On October 11th he had a painful but, as everyone thought, an unimportant accident, when during his performance his ankle sustained an injury. The incident was treated quite lightly by the Press, but was regarded more seriously by those who had other sources of information. On October 13th, two days after the accident, the gentleman already quoted had a letter from a medium, Mrs. Wood.

"Three years ago," said this ill-omened epistle, "the spirit of Dr. Hyslop said, 'The waters are black for Houdini,' and he foretold that disaster would befall him while performing before an audience in a theatre. Dr. Hyslop now says that the injury is more serious than has been reported, and that Houdini's days as a magician are over."

The sad prophecy proved to be only too true, though the injured leg was only the prelude of worse disaster. It seemed indeed to be a sign that the protective mantle which had been around him had for some reason been withdrawn. The ankle continued to pain him, though he managed for some weeks to give his accustomed show. At Montreal a member of the audience rose to protest against the violence with which he raved against Spiritualism, and very particularly against me. Such personal attacks were not to be taken too seriously, for it was part of his perfervid nature that anyone who had experiences which differed from his own was either a dupe or a scoundrel. He bore up with great bravery against the pain from which he must have continually suffered, but in less than a fortnight, while on the stage at Detroit, he completely collapsed, and was carried to that hospital from which he never emerged alive.

There were some remarkable points about his death. It seems that upon Friday, October 22nd, he was lying in his dressing-room, reading his letters. It was about five in the afternoon. He had lectured at McGill University a few days before, and with his usual affability he allowed some of the students to come in and see him. What followed may be taken verbatim from the report of one of these young men.

"'Houdini,' he says, 'was facing us and lying down on a couch at the time reading some mail, his right side nearest us.' This first-year student engaged Houdini more or less continually in a conversation whilst my friend Mr. Smilovitch continued to sketch Houdini. This student was the first to raise the question of Houdini's strength. My friend and I were not so much interested in his strength as we were in his mental acuteness, his skill, his beliefs and his personal experiences. Houdini stated that he had extraordinary muscles in his forearms, in his shoulders and in his back, and he asked all of us present to feel them, which we did.

"The first-year McGill student asked Houdini whether it was true that punches in the stomach did not hurt him. Houdini remarked rather unenthusiastically that his stomach could resist much, although he did not speak of it in superlative terms. Thereupon he gave Houdini some very hammerlike blows below the belt, first securing Houdini's permission to strike him. Houdini was reclining at the time with his right side nearest Whitehead, and the said student was more or less bending over him. These blows fell on that part of the stomach to the right of the navel, and were struck on the side nearest us, which was in fact Houdini's right side; I do not remember exactly how many blows were struck. I am certain, however, of at least four very hard and severe body blows, because at the end of the second or third blow I verbally protested against this sudden onslaught on the part of this first-year student, using the words, 'Hey there. You must be crazy, what are you doing?' or words to that effect, but Whitehead continued striking Houdini with all his strength.

"Houdini stopped him suddenly in the midst of a punch, with a gesture that he had had enough. At the time Whitehead was striking Houdini, the latter looked as though he was in extreme pain and winced as each blow was struck.

"Houdini immediately after stated that he had had no opportunity to prepare himself against the blows, as he did not think that Whitehead would strike him as suddenly as he did and with such force, and that he would have been in a better position to prepare for the blows if he had arisen from his couch for this purpose, but the injury to his foot prevented him from getting about rapidly."

There is no doubt that the immediate cause of the death was rup-
tured appendix, and it was certified as traumatic appendicitis by all
three doctors who attended him. It is, however, a very rare complaint,
one of the doctors asserting that he had never seen a case before.
When one considers how often boxers are struck violent blows in this
region, one can understand that it is not usually so vulnerable. From
the time that he reached hospital he seems to have known that he was
doomed.

Even after death strange things continued to happen which seem
to be beyond the range of chance or coincidence. Some little time before Houdini had ordered a very ornate coffin, which he proposed to
use in some sensational act. He paid no less than two thousand five
hundred dollars for it. The idea was, I believe, to have a glass face to
it and to exhibit the magician within it after it was hermetically sealed
up, for he had shown in a previous experiment an inexplicable capacity
for living without air. He carried this coffin about with him in one of
the very numerous crates in which all his apparatus was packed. After
his death all his goods were, I am told, sent on to New York. It was
found, however, that by some blunder one box had been left behind.
On examination this was found to contain the show coffin, which was
accordingly used for his burial. At that burial some curious and suggestive words were used by the presiding rabbi, Barnard Drachman. He
said: "Houdini possessed a wondrous power that he never understood,
and which he never revealed to anyone in life." Such an expression
coming at so solemn a moment from one who may have been in a special position to know must show that my speculations are not extrava-
gant or fantastic when I deal with the real source of those powers.
The rabbi's speech is to be taken with Houdini's own remark, when he
said to my wife: "There are some of my feats which my own wife does
not know the secret of." A famous Chinese conjurer who saw him perform said, "This is not a trick, it is a gift." He frequently said that his
work would die with him, and he has left no legacy of it so far as can
be seen, though it would clearly be a very valuable asset. What can
cover all these facts, save that there was some element in his power
which was peculiar to himself, and that could only point to a psychic
element—in a word, that he was a medium?

In the remarkable ceremony performed beside his coffin by his
brother-magicians, the spokesman broke a symbolic wand and said:

"The wand is broken. God touched him with a wondrous gift, and our brother used it. Now the wand is broken." It may indeed have been not mere trickery but a God-given gift which raised Houdini to such a height. And why should he not use it, if it were indeed the gift of God? I see no reason why the medium, like other God-endowed men— the painter, the poet, or the romancer—should not earn money and renown by his gift. Let him hesitate, however, before he makes rash attacks upon those who are using the same gift, and for higher ends.

Other curious points, which may possibly come within the range of coincidence, are connected with the death of Houdini. For example, there was a Mr. Gysel, who had shared in Houdini's views as to Spiritualism. He wrote thus to my friend:

"MR. FRIKELL,—
"Something happened to me in my room on Sunday night, October 24th, 1926, 10:58: Houdini had given me a picture of himself which I had framed and hung on the wall. At the above time and date the picture fell to the ground, breaking the glass. I now know that Houdini will die. Maybe there is something in these psychic phenomena after all."

To this Mr. "Frikell" adds:

"As I think back on my own experience I am inclined to agree maybe there is indeed something to the psychic phenomena after all."

His admission is the more noteworthy as I remember the day when he was a strong and intelligent opponent.

I will now turn to a consideration of the nature of Houdini's powers, and in order to appreciate the argument one has to consider the nature of some of the feats which he did actually perform. A list of these would make a considerable pamphlet, but a few typical ones may be selected. A general outline of his life, too, may not be out of place.

Houdini's real name was Eric Weiss, and he was born in 1874, in the State of Wisconsin, in one of those small towns which seem to be the real centres of American originality. He was the seventh son of a Jewish rabbi, and he has left it on record that his mother did not even know the English language. He has also left it on record that in his early youth he had some connection with mediumship, though of a most doubtful variety. He has not scrupled to confess that he eked out any powers he may have had by the expedient of reading the names upon the graves in the local cemeteries. It was a good deal later than this that he first met a true medium in the shape of Ira Davenport, the only survivor of the famous brothers whose powers amazed all England in the 'sixties, and who, in spite of all the interested claims of Maskelyne and other conjurers, were never exposed, nor even adequately imitated. I have before me as I write a letter from Houdini himself, in which he tells me:

"I was an intimate friend of Ira Erastus Davenport. I can make the positive assertion that the Davenport Brothers never were exposed. I know more about the Davenports than anyone living."

He then adds the very curious and notable sentence:

"I know for a fact that it was not necessary for them to remove their bonds in order to obtain manifestations."

When one considers that these bonds were often handcuffs or twisted copper wire, and that the manifestations occurred in many cases within a few seconds of the closing of the cabinet, this admission by one, who claims that he knows, is of very great importance. We will return to this later, after we have enumerated a few of his results.

He could, and continually did, walk straight out of any prison cell in which he might be confined. They placed him at Washington in the cell in which Guiteau, the murderer of Garfield, had been locked, but he readily emerged. In the letter from which I have already quoted, he says to me:

"I pledge my word of honour that I was never given any assistance, nor was in collusion with anyone."

This was clearly the case, for he performed the feat many times in different places, and was always searched to prove that he had no tools in his possession. Sometimes the grinning warders had hardly got out of the passage before their prisoner was at their heels. It takes some

24

credulity, I think, to say that this was, in the ordinary sense of the word, a trick.

Handcuffs might have been made of jelly, so easily did his limbs pass through them. He was heavily manacled at Scotland Yard, and placed behind a screen from over which a shower of manacles began to fall until he stepped out a free man. These things he could do in an instant. When I was lecturing at the Carnegie Hall in New York, my wife and Houdini walked down some side corridor after the lecture in order to rejoin me. They came to a padlocked door, and my wife was about to turn back. To her amazement, her companion put out his hand and picked off the locked padlock as one picks a plum from a tree. Was that a trick, or are all these talks about sleight of hand what Houdini himself would call "bunk" or "hokum"?

When Houdini was in Holland, he got the local basketmakers to weave a basket round him. Out of this he emerged. He was shut up later in a sealed paper bag and came out, leaving it intact. A block of ice was frozen round his body and he burst his way out. One who has attempted to bring his feats within the range of normal explanations tells us that he did this by "depressing his periphery as a prelude to dynamic expansion"—whatever that may mean. He was also buried six feet deep in California and emerged unhurt, though we are not told by what dynamic expansion the feat was achieved.

In Leeds he was coopered up in a cask by the brewers, but he was soon out. At Krupps' he defied the whole management, who constructed a special set of fetters for his behoof. They had no better luck than the others. He was put into the Siberian convict van at Moscow, but walked straight out of it. On December 2nd, 1906, he leaped from the Old Belle Isle Bridge at Detroit heavily handcuffed, and released himself under icy water, which would paralyse any man's limbs. On August 26th, 1907, he was thrown into San Francisco Bay with his hands tied behind his back and seventy-five pounds of ball and chain attached to his body. He was none the worse. He escaped from a padlocked United States mailbag, as many a parcel has done before him. Finally, he was manacled, tied up in a box, and dropped into the East River at New York, but lived to tell the tale.

Whatever may have been the true source of Houdini's powers—and I am not prepared to be dogmatic upon the point—I am very sure that the explanations of his fellow-conjurers do not always meet the case.

Thus we have Mr. Harry Kellock, to whose book I am indebted for much supplementary information, talking persuasively about the magician's skill with a pick-lock. He had told reporters that his method was to have a small instrument which was concealed by surgeon's plaster upon the sole of his foot. This would certainly seem to be very useful when he was lowered in a coffin to the bottom of the sea!

Of course, I am aware that Houdini really was a very skilful conjurer. All that could be known in that direction he knew. Thus he confused the public mind by mixing up things which were dimly within their comprehension with things which were beyond anyone's comprehension. I am aware also that there is a box trick, and that there is a normal handcuff and bag trick. But these are not in the same class with Houdini's work. I will believe they are when I see one of these other gentlemen thrown in a box off London Bridge. One poor man in America actually believed these explanations, and on the strength of them jumped in a weighted packing-case into a river in the Middle West; and one did so in Germany. They are there yet!

To show the difference between Houdini's methods and those by which the box trick is done by other conjurers, I will give a description of the latter by one who has all normal tricks at his finger-ends. He says:

"While the air-holes are there for ventilation they are there for another purpose, and that is that the man inside may get a catch or grip of that particular board. The first thing that is done by the man inside is to put his back up against the side next the audience and with his feet force off the board with the air-holes in it. After freeing this board, with a bit of string he lowers this board to the floor. If any obstruction comes in the way in the shape of a nail which he cannot force with his concealed lever and hammer, he cuts the nail with a fine saw. Thus his escape. The ropes are only a blind, as quite sufficient room can be got to get out between ropes. The procedure to close up again is simple. The iron nails are placed back upon the holes from which they were forced and squeezed in and knocked with a leather-covered hammer."

Such is the usual technique as described by an expert. Does anyone believe that all this could be done as I have seen Houdini do it in a little over a minute, or could one imagine it being carried out at the bottom of a river? I contend that Houdini's performance was on an utterly different plane, and that it is an outrage against common sense to think otherwise.

I will now take a single case of Houdini's powers, and of the sort of thing that he would say, in order to show the reader what he is up against if he means to maintain that these tricks had no abnormal element. The description is by my friend, Captain Bartlett, himself a man of many accomplishments, psychic and otherwise. In the course of their conversation he said to his guest:

" 'How about your box trick?'

"Instantly his expression changed. The sparkle left his eyes and his face looked drawn and haggard. 'I cannot tell you,' he said, in a low, tense voice. 'I don't know myself, and, what is more, I have always a dread lest I should fail, and then I would not live. I have promised Mrs. Houdini to give up the box trick at the end of the season, for she makes herself ill with anxiety, and for myself I shall be relieved too.'

"He stooped to stroke our cats, and to our amazement they fled from the room with their tails in the air, and for some minutes they dashed wildly up and down stairs, scattering the mats in all directions.

"After this we had an earnest talk on psychic phenomena, and he told me of strange happenings to himself, especially at the grave of his mother, to whom he was deeply attached.

"The trunk-makers of Bristol had made a challenge box from which he was billed to escape that evening. He begged me to be with him, explaining that he liked the support of a sensitive, more especially as he was feeling anxious.

"I willingly agreed, the more especially as he allowed me to bring a very observant friend, a civil engineer of repute.

"The box was made of inch planking, tongued and grooved, with double thickness at the ends. It was nailed herring-bone fashion, three-inch nails, three inches apart. Several auger holes were made at one end to admit air, and the whole thing was carefully and solidly finished. It was, as I have said, a challenge box, yet we thoroughly overhauled it and were satisfied that it contained no tricks.

"Houdini lay down in it, while the challengers climbed to the platform and nailed down the heavy top again, using three-inch nails as before. The box was then tightly roped, three men pulling on the cords. Meanwhile, Houdini inside the box called out that it was very hot, and, putting a finger through an air-hole, waggled it furiously.

27

"The box was then enclosed by a tent consisting of brass rods covered by a silken canopy.

"In ninety-five seconds Houdini was standing before his audience, breathless, and with his shirt in tatters. The boxmakers, after careful examination, in which we joined, declared that both box and roping were intact.

"Now, was Houdini's statement that he never knew how he got out of the box a mere blind, or did he employ supernormal forces and dematerialize? If I put a beetle in a bottle, hermetically sealed, and that beetle makes its escape, I, being only an ordinary human, and not a magician, can only conclude that either the beetle has broken the laws of matter, or that it possesses secrets that I should call supernormal."

I would also ask the reader to consider the following account by the late Mr. Hewat Mackenzie, one of the most experienced psychical researchers in the world. In his book, *Spirit Intercourse* (p. 86), he says:

"A small iron tank filled with water was deposited on the stage, and in it Houdini was placed, the water completely covering his body. Over this was placed an iron lid with three hasps and staples, and these were securely locked. The body was then completely dematerialized within the tank in one and a half minutes, while the author stood immediately over it. Without disturbing any of the locks Houdini was transferred from the tank direct to the back of the stage front, dripping with water and attired in the blue jersey-suit in which he entered the tank. From the time that he entered it to the time that he came to the front only one and a half minutes had elapsed.

"While the author stood near the tank during the dematerialization process a great loss of physical energy was felt by him, such as is usually felt by sitters in materializing séances who have a good stock of vital energy, as in such phenomena a large amount of energy is required. . . . This startling manifestation of one of Nature's profoundest miracles was probably regarded by most of the audience as a very clever trick."

In other words, in Mr. Mackenzie's opinion the audience was successfully bluffed by the commercialization of psychic power. It is remarkable and most suggestive that in this case, as in the Bristol one already given, Houdini was anxious that some psychic from whom he could draw strength should stand near him.

Can any reasonable man read such an account as this and then dismiss the possibility which I suggest as fantastic? It seems to me that the fantasy lies in refusing its serious consideration.

A point which is worth considering is, that even if we grant that enormous practice and natural advantages might conceivably give a man a facility in one direction which might appear preternatural, these feats of Houdini cover a larger range than could be accounted for by any one aptitude. This consideration becomes stronger still when one sees that his powers really covered the whole field of what we usually associate with physical mediumship in its strongest form, and can be covered so far as I can see by no other explanation whatever.

His friend Mr. Bernard Ernst, a well-known and very level-headed lawyer of New York, told me that on one occasion upon the veranda of his own country house at Long Island, Houdini proposed a séance. When hands were laid upon the table it began to rise up in the air. As Mrs. Houdini was present, Ernst took it for granted at first that the hands or feet were used to produce the effect. On examination, however, in good light he found that this was not so, and that there were no steel rods up the sleeve, which is a fraudulent method occasionally used. The feat appeared to him—and he is himself an experienced conjurer—to be clearly preternatural. Houdini himself rebuked a tendency towards levity upon the part of the company, and treated the matter with great gravity.

Now let us take the case of the séance which he gave to President Roosevelt—a bogus séance according to Houdini. It was on board the *Imperator* in June 1910. It followed the lines of the usual slate phenomenon as practised by many mediums, honest and otherwise. The written question, folded and sealed, is placed between the folding slates, and the answer is found upon one side of the slate when they are opened. Roosevelt wrote the question, "Where was I last Christmas?" folded, sealed in an envelope, and placed it between the slates with his own hand. When the slates were opened a map of the South American journey of Roosevelt was found to be drawn, with the legend "Near the Andes." The President was naturally greatly amazed and Houdini refused to give any explanation, though had it been a mere trick and there was no reason for secrecy, it would have been most natural that he should have explained it to so important a person, in order to show how easily fraudulent mediums can operate.

Long afterwards he did give an explanation, which is so incredible that I would take it as an extreme example of that contempt which Houdini had for the public intelligence, taking it for granted that they would swallow without question anything which he might put before them. To condense a long story which the curious may find on pages 244-6 of Kellock's very readable book, the "explanation" ran thus:

He knew that the President would be aboard and he received advance information about the South American travels from friends on the *Daily Telegraph,* which he made note of in case there should be a séance on board. So far we are on understandable ground. He suggested that such a séance should be held, and had the slates prepared. This also we may pass. He then asked for written questions from the passengers, and himself wrote several, "Where did I spend last Christmas?" which he placed upon the top of the pile. We are still on more or less solid ground, presuming that the passengers were so dense as not to see the change of slates from the one which they examined to the prepared one. But now comes the fatal link in the chain. He claims that, "no telepathy or thought-transference being involved," the President *by pure chance* asked the very question for which these elaborate preparations had been made. People will believe this, and yet accuse Spiritualists of credulity. Can anyone who has the least conception of what is probable or possible accept such an explanation? It is only in psychic and preternatural (not supernatural) regions that such things really do become commonplace.

Again, a friend reports:

"One day a sceptic called upon him. Houdini read the man's hand, prognosticated his future, and pronounced his past from a mere reading of his face, having only been told the day of his birth. This was done with an accuracy and vividness which astonished the subject."

This sounds like possible clairvoyance, but is hardly in the repertoire of the conjurer.

There were many indications that Houdini possessed that psychic sensibility which is the groundwork of mediumship, though it really indicates, in my opinion, an unusual degree of soul power in the subject itself, without necessarily implying any outside assistance. All thought-reading seems to come under this category. On one occasion Pulitzer, the famous proprietor of the *New York World,* had been interested in the telepathic results obtained by Professor Gilbert Murray in England. Houdini dashed in, in his usual impetuous fashion, and claimed that he could duplicate them. A committee assembled in his own house, and put him to the test, they sitting on the ground floor, and he being locked up in a room at the top of the house, with the door guarded. Out of four tests he got three more or less correctly. When asked for an explanation he refused to answer, save to say that it was "scientific trickery." As usual he took it for granted that the Press and public would readily accept his explanation, and experience showed that he was right.

If once the mind is adjusted to the false assumption that psychic powers do not exist, then all reasoning power seems to become atrophied, as is the case in all bigoted religions. As an example it was said, and is said, again and again, "How absurd for Doyle to attribute possible psychic powers to a man who himself denies them!" Is it not perfectly evident that if he did not deny them his occupation would have been gone for ever? What would his brother-magicians have to say to a man who admitted that half his tricks were done by what they would regard as illicit powers? It would be "exit Houdini."

Now, having considered some of Houdini's inexplicable powers, let us turn to his direct relations with Spiritualism.

PART II

In public, as is notorious, he posed as the uncompromising foe of Spiritualism. It is useless to pretend that it was only the fake medium that he was after. We are all out after that scoundrel, and ready to accept any honest help in our search for him. Houdini wrote in the *Christian Register* of July, 1925:

"Tell the people that all I am trying to do is to save them from being tricked in their grief and sorrows, and to persuade them to leave Spiritualism alone and take up some genuine religion."

Thus his attack was a general one upon the whole cult.

But this was not in the least his attitude in private. I suppose that there are few leaders of the movement, and few known mediums, who have not letters of his taking the tone that he was a sympathetic in-

31

quirer who needed but a little more to be convinced. His curious mentality caused him to ignore absolutely the experiences of anyone else, but he seemed to be enormously impressed if anything from an outside source came in his own direction. On one occasion he showed me a photograph which he had taken in California. "I believe it to be the only genuine spirit photograph ever taken!" he cried. To my mind, it was a very doubtful one, and one which no sane Spiritualist would have passed for a moment. But, in any case, if his was, as he claimed, genuine, why should he put down all others to fraud? He had another which he showed me with some disgust, but which seemed to me to be capable of a real psychic explanation, however unlikely. The sensitive film had been torn lengthways right down the plate, just as a sharp nail would have done. He assured me that he had put it into the carrier quite intact. It might, of course, have been some singular accident, or it might conceivably have been a sign of the same sort of disapproval, which was a possible explanation of the gravel-throwing in the music-hall of Boston.

His experience with decent mediums was exceedingly limited. He sat several times with Eva during the abortive investigation by the London Psychical Research Society. He wrote to me at the time, saying: "I found it highly interesting." There was no question of any exposure, and he admitted that he saw ectoplasm both come and go without being able to explain it. I believe that he once—and only once—sat with that great voice medium, Mrs. Wriedt, on which occasion nothing at all occurred, as will happen with all honest mediums, but does not happen with conjurers. There was certainly no talk of any exposure. He never sat with Miss Besinnet, nor with Mrs. Pruden, nor with Jonson of Pasadena, nor with Hope, nor with Mrs. Deane, nor with Evan Powell, nor Phoenix, nor Sloane. He claimed to have exposed P. L. O. Keeler, a medium whom I have heard quoted, but of whom I have no personal experience. Speaking generally, it may be said that his practical experience, save with a class of people whom a decent Spiritualist would neither use nor recommend, was very limited. His theoretical knowledge of the subject was also limited, for though he possessed an excellent library, it was, when I inspected it, neither catalogued nor arranged. I am told that his library was eventually put upon a more satisfactory basis, but I speak of it as I saw it. His book, *A Magician among the Spirits*, is full of errors of fact, and never for a moment did he show any appreciation of the higher religious claims of the movement.

In spite of this very limited basis, he gave the public the impression that his knowledge was profound. To one reporter he said that he had attended ten thousand séances. I pointed out at the time that this would mean one a day for thirty years. His accusations against Spiritualists were equally wild. A man, named Frank Macdowell, committed a peculiarly atrocious murder at Clearwater in Florida. Houdini broadcast the fact that it was due to spirit teaching. Fortunately, a resolute Spiritualist, Mr. Elliot Hammond, went into the matter, and showed clearly that the murderer gave his complete disbelief in life after death to have been at the root of his actions. Spiritualism would have saved him.

I repeat that Houdini's attitude in private was quite different to what it was in public. At one time we had him really converted without the slightest intention of causing such a result. It was at Atlantic City, in 1922. He had spoken in a touching manner of his mother, so my wife, who has the great gift of inspired writing—that is, of writing which appears to be quite disconnected from her own mentality—tried to see if she could get any message for him. It was done at my suggestion, and I well remember that my wife needed much persuasion. We had no sooner assembled in our quiet sitting-room than the power came, and the medium began to write with breathless and extraordinary speed, covering sheet after sheet, which I tore off and threw across to Houdini at the other side of the table. We gathered that it was a moving and impassioned message to her son from the dead mother. He asked a mental question of his mother without speech, and the medium's hand instantly wrote what he admitted to be an answer. Houdini was deeply moved, and there is no question that at the time he entirely accepted it.

When we met him two days later in New York, he said to us: "I have been walking on air ever since." I published the incident in my *American Adventure,* so that he had to explain it away to fit it into his anti-Spiritualistic campaign. The line of criticism which he took was that it could not have been from his mother, since a cross was put upon the top of the paper, and she was a Jewess. If he had cared to inquire we could have shown him that the medium *always* puts a cross on the top of her paper, as being a holy symbol. We consider that such

33

exercises are, in the highest degree, religious. That is a complete answer to the objection.

His second criticism was that the letter was in English. This was plausible, but shows an ignorance of psychic methods. If a medium were in complete trance, it might well be possible to get an unknown tongue through her. Such cases are not very rare; but when the medium is not in trance, but writing by inspiration, it is the flood of thought and of emotion which strikes her, and has to be translated by her in her own vocabulary as best she can. As an illustration, I have notes of a case where two mediums in the same room both got an inspired message at the same moment. They each wrote down the same sense, but the wording was quite different. Thus the second criticism falls to the ground. In any case, one would imagine that he would have nothing but respect and gratitude for one who tried to help him, with no conceivable advantage to herself. No sign of this appears. It is the same queer mental twist which caused him first to take the name of the great Frenchman, and then to write a whole book, *The Unmasking of Houdin,* to prove that he was a fraud.

But there was another very curious and suggestive incident in connection with that sitting at Atlantic City. As Houdini, much moved, rose from the table, he took up the pencil, and, bending to the papers, he said: "I wonder if I could do anything at this!" The pencil moved and he wrote one word. Then he looked up at me and I was amazed, for I saw in his eyes that look, impossible to imitate, which comes to the medium who is under influence. The eyes look at you, and yet you feel that they are not focused upon you. Then I took up the paper. He had written upon it one word, "Powell." My friend, Ellis Powell, had just died in England, so the name had a meaning. "Why, Houdini," I cried, "Saul is among the prophets! You are a medium." Houdini had a poker-face and gave nothing away as a rule, but he seemed to me to be disconcerted by my remark. He muttered something about knowing a man called "Powell" down in Texas, though he failed to invent any reason why that particular man should come back at that particular moment. Then, gathering up the papers, he hurried from the room. It is probable that at that moment I had surprised the master secret of his life—a secret which even those who were nearest to him had never quite understood. Each fact alone may be capable of explanation, but when a dozen facts all point in the same direction, then surely there is a case to answer.

I have said that the Houdini mentality was the most obscure that I have ever known. Consider this manifestation of it. My wife and I were, as I have shown, endeavouring to help him, with no possible motive save to give him such consolation as we could, since he was always saying that he wished to get in touch with his mother. Such consolation has often been given to others. Even if we suppose, for argument's sake, that we were mistaken in our views, we were, as he often admits, in dead earnest. Then, as we rose, he wrote down the name Powell, which meant much to me. If it was not written under psychic influence, why should he write anything at all, since no one asked him to do so? He saw the difficulty when he had to explain it away, so in his book he says that it was a "deliberate mystification" upon his part, and that he wrote it entirely of his own volition. Thus by his own showing, while we were honest with him, he was playing what I will charitably describe as a practical joke upon us. Is it any wonder that we look back at the incident with some bitterness? He does not attempt to explain how it was that out of all his friends the name that he wrote was the very one which might well have wished to come through to me. There is a limit to coincidence.

It is a curious fact that neither my wife nor I knew what was in the mother's letter until I read it in his book. It was written so swiftly that the medium, in her half-unconscious state, could at best only have a very vague idea of its purport, while I never even glanced at it. Now that I read it, it seems to me to be a very beautiful letter, full of love and of longing. As I have explained, the thoughts are given and are largely translated by the medium. Therefore, there are some sentences in which I can recognize my wife's style of expression, but the greater part of it is far more fervid—one might almost say more Oriental—than anything I have known my wife do. Here is a short extract:

"Oh, my darling, my darling, thank God at last I am through. I've tried, oh, so often. Now I am happy. Of course, I want to talk to my boy, my own beloved boy. . . . My only shadow has been that my beloved one has not known how often I have been with him all the while. . . . I want him only to know that—that—I have bridged the gulf—that is what I wanted—oh, so much. Now I can rest in peace."

It was a long and very moving message and bore every internal sign of being genuine. There is no question at all in my mind that Houdini was greatly shaken at the time and for some days afterwards. His objections were all afterthoughts in order to save the situation.

In the account of the matter which Houdini gave, he lays stress upon the fact that Mrs. Houdini had spoken to my wife the night before as to Houdini's affairs, with many details as to his habits when with his mother. Now if the message had really come from my wife's subconscious self I think it is certain that some of this information would have come through. I have known this to happen in the case of perfectly honest mediums and for this reason it is better never to tell a medium anything at all before a séance. A blank slate is the best to write upon. In the long message, however, which my wife gave there was no trace at all of the knowledge which she had normally gained, and which could have been used so effectively if anyone had been so wicked as to play a trick. This is, I think, a very clear sign that the message was not subconscious but did really come from the source it claimed. Houdini's objection that the mother made no mention of the fact that it was her own birthday has no relevancy. What are birthdays on the other side? It is the death day which is the real birthday. In her rush of joy and emotion why should she pause to mention such a fact? The method in which Houdini tried to explain away, minimize and contort our attempt at consolation, which was given entirely at his own urgent request and against my wife's desire, has left a deplorable shadow in my mind which made some alteration in my feelings for him. Conscious as I was of his many excellent and wonderful qualities, such incidents took the edge off my sympathies, and put a strain upon our friendship.

When my friend, the late Miss Scatcherd, was in New York, some years ago, she saw a good deal of Houdini, and got, I fancy, as nearly into his complete confidence as anyone could do. To her, as to me, he showed no animosity to psychic things, but, on the contrary, he was eager to show her the one and only true medium whom he had discovered in America. Miss Scatcherd was not, I gather, much impressed by his find, having known many better ones. She did not fail, however, to point out to him that in admitting the one medium he had really given away his whole case, and agreed that the Spiritualists had a solid foundation for their cult. She then accused him of being a powerful medium himself, for she was a strong sensitive, and all her psychic powers told her that he was the same. She also scolded him in her charming, good-natured way for having behaved shamefully in the "Margery" case, which he did not deny. The climax came, however, when, far out on the Atlantic, she received the following wireless message:

"From a sensitive to a sensitive. Wishing you a pleasant voyage.—Houdini."

A sensitive is a medium, and what is the logic of denouncing all mediums as frauds from the public platforms, and at the same time declaring in a telegram that you are one yourself?

Let us now follow a fresh line of thought. There can be no question at all, to anyone who has really weighed the facts, that Ira Davenport was a true medium. Apart from the evidence of thousands of witnesses, it is self-evident that he could at any time, by announcing himself and his brother as conjurers, and doing his unique performances as tricks, have won fame and fortune. This would seem a dreadful thing to do from the point of view of a good Spiritualist, and the Davenports went to the last possible limit by leaving the source of their powers to the audience to determine. Houdini has endeavoured to take advantage of this and to make out that Ira admitted in his old age that his feats were tricks. To clear away such an idea, I append the following letter, written by Ira in 1868 to *The Banner of Light*:

"It is singular that any individual, sceptic or Spiritualist, could believe such statements after fourteen years of the most bitter persecution, culminating in the riots of Liverpool, Huddersfield, and Leeds, where our lives were placed in imminent peril by the fury of brutal mobs, our property destroyed, all because we would not renounce Spiritualism and declare ourselves jugglers when threatened by the mob and urged to do so. In conclusion, we denounce all such statements as base falsehoods."

We happen to be particularly well informed about the Davenports, for, apart from long statements from many well-known people who examined them, there are three books by people who knew them well, and who could not possibly have been deceived had they been swindlers.

The smaller book, by Orrin Abbott, covers the early days, and the author tells how he was intimate with the brothers when they were little boys, and how at that time he had every opportunity of observing and testing their wonderful powers. These seem, as is often the case with mediums, to have been stronger in childhood than in later life, the power of levitation being one which Abbott witnessed, but which is not recorded of them elsewhere. The second and fullest is Dr. Nicol's biography, while the third and most valuable is found in the *Supramundane Facts* of the Rev. J. B. Ferguson. Ferguson was a man of very high character, with a notable record behind him, and he travelled with the Davenports during their tour in England. He was with them at all hours of the day and night, and he has left it on record that their experiences when in private were quite as wonderful as anything that the public ever saw. It is notable that these well-attested feats included not only the instant freedom from ropes, however carefully fastened and sealed by the spectators, but also, on occasion, the freedom from handcuffs or twisted wire, and the power of opening locked doors. In a word, the Davenport powers were the Houdini powers, save that the latter had physical strength and agility which may have helped him to extend them.

My argument now begins to emerge. If it be true that the Davenports were real mediums (and let the inquirer really read their record before he denies it),[1] and if Houdini produced exactly similar results, which have in each case been inexplicable to their contemporaries, then is it conceivable that they were produced in entirely different ways? If Ira Davenport was a medium, then there is a strong primâ facie case that Houdini was a medium too. Now we come upon some explanation of the cryptic saying of the rabbi by the graveside: "He possessed a wondrous power that he never understood, and which he never revealed to anyone in life." What could that power be, save what we have called the power of the medium?

A singular incident is narrated by Mrs. Houdini and is incorporated in Mr. Kellock's biography. Shortly after his marriage, Houdini took his girl wife and his brother to a lonely place, where he halted them upon a bridge at midnight. When the hour came he made them both raise their hands in the air and said to them, "Beatrice, Dash, raise your

[1] It will be found epitomized in my *History of Spiritualism* (Cassell).

hands to heaven and swear that both of you will be true to me. Never betray me in any way, so help you God!" I would not put too much stress upon this incident. It may have been the considered act of one who already had some strange and secret knowledge which he foresaw might be used in the future and might be surprised by those around him.

I would not, in probing this difficult problem, pass too lightly over the considered words of the rabbi, that he had a wondrous power and did not himself understand it. This phrase fits very exactly into what has been stated to me by those who were nearest to him in life. "If it was so, he did not know it," they have answered when I hinted at my conclusions. It seems hard to comprehend, and yet there may be something in this view. He was not a clear thinker, and he had no logical process in his mind. That surely is evident when in the same breath he denies all mediumship and claims to have discovered the greatest medium in America; or when he scoffs at spirit pictures but brings me a very indifferent one which he had taken himself. Imagine that such a man finds himself one minute inside a box; there is an interval of semi-trance during which his mind is filled with a vague feeling of confused effort, and then he finds himself outside the box. There is no obvious intervention of spirits, or of any outside force, but it just happens so. He has the same power in emerging from fetters, but he has no sort of philosophy by which he can explain such things. If we could imagine such a very strange and unlikely state of things as that, it would, at least, have the merit that it would give some sort of honest and rational explanation of a good deal which at present is dark. It is no unusual thing for a medium to fail to understand his own results, but it would certainly seem almost incredible that anyone could have such results for many years and never correlate them with the experience of others. I, as his former friend, would welcome such an explanation if it could be sustained.

But how does the good rabbi know that he did not understand it? Only one man could say with authority, but he has passed away with closed lips, leaving, however, many signs behind for those who have the wit to follow them. There is one thing certain, and that is that the fate of the Davenports must have been a perpetual warning to Houdini. They had been ruined and hunted off the stage because it was thought that their claim was psychic. If his powers were to be drawn from that source, and if he were to avoid a similar fate, then his first and fundamental law must be that it be camouflaged in every possible way, and that no one at all should know his secret. If this be granted, a great many disconnected points become at once a connected whole. We see what he meant when he said that his own wife did not know how he produced his effects. We understand the voice of which he spoke. We comprehend dimly the unknown power of the rabbi. We can even imagine that a campaign against mediums, fortified by the knowledge that false mediums do exist, would be an excellent smoke-screen, though probably he had never thought out what view the unseen powers might take of such a transaction, any more than he calculated upon the interposition of Walter in the case of the conspiracy against the Crandons. I cannot say that all this is certain. I can only say that it covers the facts as I know them.

Of course, I know that he had a trick-box. I know also who constructed it, and the large amount that he paid for it. When I know also that he could do his escapes equally well in any local box, I am not inclined to attach much importance to the matter. He was a very astute man, and what he did he would do thoroughly, but he became too careless in his methods as he found he could do them with impunity.

Houdini is curiously contradictory in his account of the methods of Davenport. In his book *A Magician among the Spirits*, he says:

"Their method of releasing themselves was simple. When one extended his feet the other drew his in, thus securing slack enough in the wrist rope to permit working their hands out of the loops. The second brother was released by reversing the action."

But, as I have shown, in a letter to me he said:

"I know for a positive fact that it was not essential for them to release the bonds in order to obtain manifestations."

So the previous explanation would seem to have been a fake in order to conceal the real one.

In another letter he says:

"I am afraid I cannot say that all of their work was accomplished by spirits."

The "all" is suggestive. I would be the last to suggest that all of Davenport's or indeed that all of Houdini's work could be due to spirits. For that matter, we have to remember that we are ourselves spirits here and now, and that a man may very well be producing psychic effects without going beyond his own organism. It is in this sense that I suspect the Houdini results as being psychic, and I do not at all insist upon the interposition of outside forces. The two things are not far apart, however, and very easily slide into each other. There is, I hold, the medium's use of his own power, there is a vague borderland, and there is a wide world beyond where his power is used by forces outside himself. I am convinced, for example, that raps may be produced voluntarily by a medium by a psychic effort, and I am equally convinced that at another stage these same raps may be used for purposes quite beyond his knowledge or control.

It is possible for a man to be a very powerful medium all his life, to use that power continually, and yet never to realize that the gifts he is using are those which the world calls mediumship? If that be indeed possible, then we have a solution of the Houdini enigma. One who knew him well and worked with him often wrote to me as follows:

"Often he would get a difficult lock. I would stand by the cabinet and hear him say: 'This is beyond me.' After many minutes, when the audience became restless, I would say, 'If there is anything in this belief in Spiritism why don't you call on them to assist you?' And before many minutes had passed Houdini had mastered the lock. He never attributed this to psychic help. He just knew that that particular instrument was the one to open that lock, and so he did all his tricks."

It is only fair to state, however, that this correspondent, who was in a good position to know, would not admit the mediumship. And yet if "that particular instrument" was, as stated, an appeal to spirits, it seems difficult to claim that the result was natural.

I would not limit my hypothesis to the idea that it was only when he met the Davenports that he first developed these strange powers. He seems only to have met Ira in 1909, and he had certainly done many marvellous feats himself before then. But the history and object-lesson of the Davenports must have been well known to him, and have shown him what to avoid.

41

In putting forward such a view as I have here expressed it is natural that a critic should demand that I should show that similar results to those of Houdini have actually been produced by psychic power. Of this there can be no possible doubt upon the part of anyone who has studied the subject. I have already mentioned the case of the Davenports who were so badly treated by the English mob, and so maligned by Maskelyne and other English conjurers who produced a feeble imitation of their results and called it an exposure. They freed themselves with the greatest ease from metal bands as well as from the tightest ligatures. Such results can only be obtained by the passage of matter through matter—of the wrist for example through the metal—and though such a thing may seem inconceivable to the prosaic scientist of to-day, he would have pronounced wireless or flying to be equally impossible a generation or so in the past. We seem to need no spirit intervention here, but to be within the region of the latent powers of the human organism in peculiarly constituted individuals. There is, I believe, a constructive and a destructive power in thought alone which is akin to that "faith which moves mountains." What sort of vibration it can be which is shot out from the human brain and separates for a moment the molecules of that solid object towards which it is directed I do not know, but the results are clear and perhaps in the near future the cause may become equally so. From personal observation I have assured myself that mediums in sealed bonds can cast those bonds, walk about the room, and be found later with the sealed bonds as before. If they could get out by a trick I see no way in which they could get back. I am forced, therefore, to predicate the existence of such a dematerializing and reconstructing force, which would amply cover most of the phenomena both of the Davenports and of Houdini. Such a force was demonstrated also in the experiments which were made with Slade by Zöllner and three other German professors, and described by him in his *Transcendental Physics*. In this book many instances, closely observed, of the passage of matter through matter were recorded, accompanied by the interesting observation that the phenomenon was accompanied often by heat and a strong smell of burning.[2] Bellachini, the Court conjurer, deposed that the results he saw were out of the region of conjuring altogether.[3] But suppose that Slade had

[2] *Transcendental Physics,* by Prof. Zöllner (English translation), p. 113.
[3] *Vide* appendix of the above book.

gone round the world doing such things and allowing people to believe that they were tricks, while confusing the public by mixing them up with real tricks, would not his position have been very close to that of Houdini?

We come, however, upon a more advanced class of phenomenon when we consider the case of the passage of a human body through a solid obstacle and its reassembly on the other side. If I can show that such cases have upon most unquestionable evidence occurred then I shall have got a possible line upon Houdini's performance. In the April number of *Psychic Science* there is the report by an American lady, Mrs. Hack, of the phenomena at a circle sitting in the Castle Millesimo, which is near Genoa. Mrs. Hack was herself present, as were the well-known Professor Bozzano, and other first-class witnesses. The Marquis Centurione Scotto, the owner of the castle, was one of the company. Suddenly in the midst of the proceedings he vanished from his chair. His friends were horrified. They searched the room and the castle, but he was gone. Finally, after hours of agitation he was found in a deep trance in an outhouse, which was separated by several locked doors from the main building. He was led back; and had no recollection how he had got there. Such in a few words is the gist of a case which was closely observed and fully reported. In it a human body is passed through several solid obstacles and reassembled on the other side. How does this differ from the passage of Houdini's body through wooden planks, brick walls, paper bags, glass tanks, or whatever else was used to confine him?[4]

In Mr. Campbell Holms' book, *The Facts of Psychic Science*, which is, and will be always, a most exact and valuable book of reference, there are a number of cases given where people have been transported through solid objects. Inexperienced and foolish people may jeer, but they will find it easier to do so than to refute the evidence. For example, upon June 3rd, 1871, Mrs. Guppy was floated from her own house in Highbury, and appeared upon the table of a room at 61 Lambs Conduit Street, where a séance was being held behind locked doors. A document was signed by the eleven sitters to testify to the fact and they had no possible object in perjuring themselves about the matter. Mrs.

[4] These remarkable experiences are more fully described in Mrs. Hack's *Modern Psychic Mysteries* (Rider).

Guppy said that the last thing she could remember was sitting with her friend Miss Neyland. That lady deposed that Mrs. Guppy had suddenly vanished from her sight. Four of the sitters accompanied Mrs. Guppy home and heard what her friend had to say. It is difficult to find any flaw in such evidence and it would certainly have been conclusive in a court of law had it been a criminal case. But surely such a transposition is more remarkable than any of Houdini's, and had she done similar things in public her reputation would have been similar to his own.

In another case, that of Mr. Henderson, a photographer, quoted by Mr. Campbell Holms and described in the *Spiritual Magazine* of 1874 (p. 22), no less than ten persons saw him vanish from a room, while nine others deposed to his arrival almost instantaneously at a point more than a mile distant. The idea that these nineteen witnesses can be disregarded is surely an impossible one, and yet here again we have evidence of the possibility by psychic means of passing a human body through solid obstacles by a process of dematerialization and reassembly. I could quote a number of other cases, but the sum of it all is that Houdini's exploits, which are inexplicable in any other way, come into line at once if we compare them with other well-attested examples of psychic power. When one adds this evidence to the various other indications of similar powers which I have assembled here, the case seems to me to be greatly strengthened.

That Houdini's performances were on a different level from those of other magicians is shown by the fact that men who took a pride in fathoming such problems, and who were usually successful, were utterly foiled in their attempts to explain them in any reasonable way. Thus Mr. H. L. Adam, an English journalist who is an expert in such matters, writes to me that he could understand much that was done by Maskelyne and others, but

"I have never been able to discover anything about Houdini's tricks. Why? I have stood quite near him on the stage during the performances of many of his tricks, but it was like looking at a brick wall, so impenetrable were they. I remember on one occasion, while Houdini was waiting at the side of the stage ready for his 'turn,' he sat in a chair, threw his head back, closed his eyes, and appeared plunged in the profoundest meditations. A few moments before he had been talking confidentially to me. After the lapse of perhaps ten minutes, he 'came to' and continued his conversation with me as though nothing had intervened."

"Houdini once suggested to me that he should, by way of advertisement, profess to 'give away' his handcuff trick, which I was to publish. But it struck me that the volunteered so-called explanation, which included a hidden key, was too feeble to be convincing, and it was never developed. This was the nearest approach he ever came to discussing any of his secrets with me."

Here again in that trance-like condition before a performance we seem to get a glimpse of some psychic influence.

Houdini continually admitted that there were psychic things which he could not understand. I would say in parenthesis that one may be a strong medium oneself and yet have very small understanding of other people's phenomena. That was conspicuous in the case of D. D. Home. Here is a Houdini story told by Don Ryan[5]:

"Houdini had gone in a spiritualist church in Los Angeles, taking a camera-man, who carried a camera concealed. They made themselves inconspicuous till the witching hour at which the ghost was accustomed to walk. The hour came and with it the spirit. The leader of the group was holding conversation with the invisible spirit when the camera was trained on the spot without the knowledge of anybody save Houdini and his photographer.

"The developed plate which Houdini showed me revealed a well-defined transparent human figure draped in white.

" 'I can't explain it and I don't know what to think of it,' said Houdini that day, and I could see that the thing had made a decided impression on him.

" 'It's no more astonishing than your staying under water for an hour and a half in a lead-lined coffin,' I told him.

" 'Ah,' replied Houdini, 'but I know how that is done.' "

The attempts upon the part of his brother-magicians to give some sort of explanation of Houdini's feats only serve to deepen the mystery. Mr. Howard Thurston, for whose opinion I have respect, for he seemed to me to be the only American conjurer who had some real accurate knowledge of psychic matters, says that his feats all come within the power of advanced conjuring. I know that feats with the same name do so, but I venture to express the opinion that such feats as Houdini did have never been explained and are in an altogether different class. So too,

[5] *New York American*, February 11th, 1928.

Mr. Will Goldston, who is well known and respected as an authority on conjuring, has actually described in a book how they are done. Here again he seems to me to be describing the accepted methods, which by no means covers Houdini's results. To show the inadequacy of Mr. Goldston's "explanations"[6] he says in talking of the escape under water, "Without giving away his secrets I may say that he was always practically out of the box before it reached the water." Considering that the screwed and corded box was in full sight of hundreds of spectators as it sank beneath the waves, it is difficult to accept such a solution as this. I admit that I am at a disadvantage when opposed to the technical knowledge of such men as Goldston and Thurston, but on the other hand I have my own technical and expert knowledge of psychic possibilities, and I put up a case for consideration and discussion.

He had, as already stated, a sitting with the medium Eva, and under the stringent and very deterrent conditions imposed by the London Psychical Research Society, which will be found described in their unsatisfactory and self-contradictory report, he did seem to have made acquaintance with ectoplasm in its very humblest form. He says in a letter to me written the next morning (June 22nd, 1920):

"They made Eva drink a cup of coffee and eat some cake (I presume to fill her up with some food-stuff), and after she had been sewn into the tights, and a net over her face, she manifested.

1. "Some froth-like substance, inside of net, 'twas long, about five inches, she said it was elevated, but none of us four watchers saw it 'elevate.'
2. "A white plaster-looking affair over her right eye.
3. "Something that looked like a small face, say four inches in circumference. Was terra-cotta coloured, and Dingwall, who held her hand, had the best look at the 'object.'
4. "Some substance, froth-like, exuding from her nose, and Baggeley and Fielding say it protrudes from her nose, but Dingwall and I are positive that it was inside of net and was not extending from her nose, as I had the best view from two different places I deliberately took advantage to see just what it was.
5. "Medium asked permission to remove something in her mouth, show her hands empty, and took out what appeared to be a rubberish substance, which she disengaged, showed us plainly, we held the electric torch, all saw it

[6] Sunday Express, November 7th, 1926.

plainly, when presto! it vanished. It was a surprise effect indeed! The séance started at 7:30 and lasted past midnight.

"We went over the notes, and no doubt you will get a full report. I found it highly interesting."

It will be found from these extracts that when faced with facts his attitude was very different from what his public utterances would lead one to expect.

Be his mystery what it may, Houdini was one of the most remarkable men of whom we have any record, and he will live in history with such personalities as Cagliostro, the Chevalier D'Eon, and other strange characters. He had many outstanding qualities, and the world is the poorer for his loss. As matters stand, no one can say positively and finally that his powers were abnormal, but the reader will, I hope, agree with me that there is a case to be answered.

II
THE SHADOWS
ON THE SCREEN

THERE IS NOTHING more wonderful, more incredible, and at the same time, as it seems to me, more certain, than that past events may leave a record upon our surroundings which is capable of making itself felt, heard, or seen for a long time afterwards. I have put the impressions in the order of their frequency, for it is more common to feel the past than to hear it and more common to hear it than to see it. Houses which are haunted by vague noises are more common than those which possess apparitions, and families have been persecuted for years by poltergeists who have never once caught a glimpse of their tormentors.

A sensitive mind is easily affected in any place where there has been recent trouble. A lady of my acquaintance called recently upon the matron of a hospital and found that she was not in her room. "Mrs. Dodson has gone out," said the nurse. "Has she had bad news?" "Yes, she has just had a wire that her husband is very ill." How did my friend know that there had been bad news? She felt it by a sinking of her own heart as she entered the room, before the nurse had arrived. "Telepathy!" says the parrot. Well, if telepathy can be stretched to mean that a thought or emotion can not only be flashed from brain to brain, but that it can remain stationary for an hour and then impress itself upon any sensitive who approached it, then I will not quarrel with the world. But if for an hour why not for a year, and if for a year why not for a century? There is a record on the etheric screen so that it may retain indefinitely some intimate and lasting change which marks and can even faintly reproduce the emotion which a human being had endured within it.

I had a friend who lived in a century-old house. His wife, who was sensitive, was continually aware of a distinct push when she came down the stairs, always occurring upon the same step. Afterwards it was discovered that an old lady who had formerly lived in the house received a playful push from some frolicsome child, and lost her balance, falling down the stairs. It is not necessary to believe that some hobgoblin lingered upon that stair continually repeating the fatal action. The probable explanation seems to be that the startled mind of the old woman as she felt herself falling left some permanent effect behind it which could still be discerned in this strange fashion.

But on what could an impression be left? An impression of such a nature becomes a material thing and implies a material nexus, however subtle. So far as we know there are only two things there, the air and the ether. The air is a mobile thing and could not carry a permanent impression. But is the ether a mobile thing? It is pictured as a most delicate medium with vibrating currents flowing in it, but it seems to me that a most tenuous jelly with quivers and thrills would be a closer analogy. We could conceive the whole material universe embedded in and interpenetrated by this subtle material, which would not necessarily change its position since it is too fine for wind or any coarser material to influence it. I feel that I am rushing in where even Lodges fear to tread, but if it should prove to be as I suggest then we should have that permanent screen on which shadows are thrown. The block of ether upon the stairs is the same that it always was, and so conveys the impression from the past.

Invisible air records of this sort would explain many things which are now inexplicable. Men of strong nerve have been known to be terrified in certain localities without being able to give any reason. Some horror of the past, unseen by their eyes, may still have impressed their senses. One does not need to be very psychic to get the same result upon an old battlefield. I am by no means psychic myself, and yet I am conscious, quite apart from imagination, of a curious effect, almost a darkening of the landscape with a marked sense of heaviness, when

I am on an old battlefield. I have been particularly conscious of it on the scenes of Hastings and Culloden, two fights where great causes were finally destroyed and where extreme bitterness may well have filled the hearts of the conquered. The shadow still remains. A more familiar example of the same faculty is the gloom which gathers over the mind of even an average person upon entering certain houses. The most rabid agitator need not envy our nobility their stately old castles, for it is happier to spend one's life in the simplest cottage, uncontaminated by psychic disturbance, than to live in the grandest mansion which still preserves the gloomy taints that hang about rooms once perhaps the scene of cruelty or other vices.

If a sensitive is able to feel some record of a past event, then there is evidence that by an extension of this process one who is still more sensitive would actually see the person who left the impression. That it is the actual person in spirit is in most cases utterly incredible to me. That the victim of some century-old villainy should still in her ancient garments frequent in person the scene of her former martyrdom is, indeed, hard to believe. It is more credible, little as we understand the details, that some thought-form is shed and remains visible, at the spot where great mental agony has been endured. "How" and "why" are questions which will be solved by our descendants. If we could conceive that we have form within form like the skins of an onion, that the outer skin should peel off under the influence of emotion and continue a mechanical existence at that spot while the rest of the organism passed on and never even missed it, such a supposition, farcical as it appears, would match the recorded facts better than anything else I know. Each fresh discarded skin of the onion would be a fresh thought-form, and our track through life would be marked in its more emotional crisis by a long trail of such forms. Grotesque as the idea may seem, I can confidently say that the true explanation when it arrives will prove to be not less so.

Let us now take some definite examples where this thought-form of the past has manifested itself. I do not know a better case than that which is recorded by the late Miss Goodrich-Freer, a lady who combined a steady nerve and cool judgment with a temperament which was conservative to the point of incredulity. She slept in a room in Hampton Court Palace which had a record of haunting, and she tells us very clearly what occurred. No unprejudiced person could possibly read the original narrative without being absolutely convinced that the facts were even as stated.

It was a small bedroom without curtains, with one door close by the bed. It is characteristic of the lady that she spent her vigil—she had come in the hope of seeing the apparition—by reading Lord Farrer's article, "Shall we degrade our standard of value?" In spite of the reading, or possibly on account of it, she fell asleep, and was awakened some hours later by sounds of movement. It was quite dark, and some detaining force seemed to prevent her from reaching for the matches. A question received no reply. Suddenly there appeared a soft point of light in the gloom, which glowed and spread, until it became the figure of a tall, slight woman, moving slowly across the room. She stopped at the farther side and the observer was able to get a clear view of her profile. "Her face was insipidly pretty, that of a woman from thirty to thirty-five years of age, her figure slight, her dress of a dark soft material, having a full skirt and broad sash or waistband tied high up, a crossed or draped kerchief over the shoulder, sleeves which I noticed fitted very tight below the elbow, and hair which was dressed so as not to lie flat on the head." A second question addressed to this figure produced no effect. She raised her thin white hands, sank upon her knees, buried her face in the palms, and appeared to pray. Then the light went out and the scene was over. The impression left upon the observer's mind by the action and attitude was that of reproach, and yet of gentle resignation. Her own nerves were so entirely unaffected by the incident that she has left it on record that she spent part of the remainder of the night in reading Myers' *Drift of Psychical Research*.

Such an experience, and it is one of a very numerous class, can hardly be explained rationally upon any spiritual or upon any physical basis. Granting the fact, and there is no sane alternative but to grant it, we cannot conceive that this unfortunate woman has really for a century or more occupied herself in walking across a room in which some great trouble may have befallen her in her earth-life. From her appearance one would judge that she was more sinned against than sinning. Why, then, should any just dispensation condemn her to so strange, monotonous, and useless a fate? If we can conceive, however, that it is some shadow of herself which was detached in old days of trouble, and still lingers, then certainly the matter becomes more clear, if she herself is happy elsewhere. Such a shadow, like most psychic phenomena, might well seem luminous to one who, like Miss Goodrich-Freer, had herself some clairvoyant gifts. If you ask, however, why such a thought-form should only come at certain hours, I am compelled to answer that I do not know.

A similar first-hand example may be drawn from Mrs. Tweedale's book, *Ghosts I Have Seen*, which, under its popular title, contains a most extraordinary record of actual first-hand psychic experiences. Mrs. Tweedale is an admirable witness, for she, like Miss Goodrich-Freer, is herself clairvoyante, and yet retains a very sane and critical judgment, while her personal reputation and position give us every confidence in her statements. Materialists will never fairly face the obvious alternative that such firsthand accounts either mean that a person of honour has suddenly burst into a perfect orgy of objectless lying, or else that the statements are true. When a clairvoyante can clearly describe her own experiences the book becomes of great value, and I would only name Turvey's *Beginnings of Seership* among the more recent works as equalling Mrs. Tweedale's in personal knowledge.

The writer at one time lived in an old house in the West End of London. It was a winter night, and she was lying half asleep when she heard a sound as of the crackling of parchment, and opening her eyes she saw a man seated in a chair in front of the fire. He was dressed in a uniform reminiscent of Nelson's days, with brass buttons, wore powdered hair with a black bow, and was staring rigidly into the glow, while he held crumpled up in his right hand some sort of document. He was a stately and handsome figure. For some hours he sat there, the fire gleaming, when it spurted up, upon the buckles and buttons of his dress. Finally, in the small hours of the morning he vanished gradually away. Several times later the lady saw the same apparition, and it might well be argued that it was constantly there, but that its perception depended upon the condition of the clairvoyante. Finally some religious exorcism was performed in the room and the vision was not seen again.

This case clearly fits itself into the hypothesis advanced here, of a form-picture being thrown out at a time of emotion. The parchment document suggests a will or some other paper of importance which the officer has prepared or received, but which in either case may have caused him so much mental stress as he brooded over it in front of the fire that he threw this permanent record upon the screen of time. The accompaniment of appropriate sound is very general in such cases. Difficult as my hypothesis may seem, we have to remember that the only conceivable other explanations would be either that the man's self was there in front of the fire after a century of spirit-life, or that his thoughts in the spirit-world concerning an episode in his earth-life were so constant and vivid that they conjured up a picture in the room. The latter explanation might be accepted for a single episode, but when it is a constant matter, and when one remembers how many other reminiscences of earth-life such a man must have had, it is difficult to consider it seriously.

An experience which comes under the same heading is narrated by Lady Reay in the same enthralling volume. She was sleeping in an ancient dwelling with a somewhat sinister reputation, so we may admit that her mind was prepared to see a ghost. The actual form of the phantom was so definite, and so exactly similar to that seen by independent witnesses at different times in the same room, that it could hardly be a figment of the brain. She was awakened by moaning. The room was in total darkness, but at one side was a circle of light, like that thrown by a magic lantern. This seems to be the psychic illumination, as seen by Miss Goodrich-Freer in the case already quoted. Several clairvoyants who habitually see it describe it as being of a metallic yellow. In this circle of radiance was seen a woman dressed as in the Tudor period, walking round the apartment, throwing herself occasionally against the wall, like a desperate bird in a cage, and moaning terribly. There was no record, so far as I know, as to who this unhappy lady may have been, but she was seen independently before Lady Reay saw her, but without Lady Reay's knowledge, by Captain Eric Streatfield when he was a little boy. I do not understand how one can disregard such testimony as this. Such incredulity may be described as scientific caution, but to those who are really aware of the weight of evidence now existing, it must appear mere obstinacy and obtuseness. When one thinks of the importance of psychic knowledge, and compares it with that of the bending of the light from the Hyades as it passes the sun, one can but marvel at the want of proportion which exalts the physical while it neglects the spiritual.

An adventure which occurred to a friend of mine seems to come under this heading. His family had rented an old country house in which Nell Gwynne had been kept when she was the mistress of

Charles II. One evening, as he descended the stairs, he saw cross the hall a figure which was very like a family nurse, whom we will call "Nannie." He cried out "Nannie!" in surprise and followed her, but could find no trace. Inquiry proved that the servant was not in the house or in the neighbourhood. My friend amused himself by fitting up the house with as many old prints of Nell Gwynne as he could collect. One day his sister visited him, and after inspecting these pictures she exclaimed: "Have you ever observed how like Nell Gwynne is to our Nannie?" There is, of course, a chance of coincidence here, but at least there is a strong suggestion that poor Nell, wearied and miserable, with her heart aching for the bustle of town, cast off some thought-form as a permanent record of her emotion.

In all these cases there has been only one figure thrown upon the screen, but the matter becomes more complex when there is a group. This group consists in many cases of the wronger and the wronged, but as each may have been at the same pitch of emotion at the time of the deed, the theory of thought-forms being shed at such a time is not invalidated—and is, at any rate, more reasonable than to imagine that the guilty murderer and the innocent victim are involved in one common fate, which consists of an endless repetition of the tragedy which they once enacted. Such an idea seems to me a monstrous and unthinkable one.

I would choose as a good example of the composite thought-form one which was recorded some years ago in the *Wide World Magazine*, which I have every reason to believe is founded on fact, though the name given, Grace Dundas, is a pseudonym, and the events occurred twenty years ago. In this very dramatic case a lady with her children occupied a lonely house upon the Cornish coast, and was much disturbed by a ghostly visitor who passed with a heavy tread up the stairs at a certain hour of the night, disappearing into a panel in the landing. The lady had the courage to lie in wait for him, and perceived him to be a small, aged man in a shabby tweed suit, carrying his boots in his hand. He emitted "a sort of yellow luminous light." This creature ascended at 1 a.m., and emerged again at 4:30, descending the stair with the same audible tread. The lady kept the matter to herself, but a nurse who was brought to tend one of the children came screaming in the middle of the night to say that there was "a dreadful old man" in the house. She had descended to the dining-room to get some water for her patient, and had seen him seated in a chair and taking off his boots. He was seen by his own light, for she had not had time to strike a match. The lady's brother and her husband both corroborated the phenomena, and the latter went very thoroughly into the matter. He found that under the house was a cellar which opened into a cave, up which the water came at full tide. It was an ideal situation for a smuggler. That night the husband and wife kept watching the cellar, where they saw a very terrible spectacle. In a light resembling that of the moon they were aware of two elderly men engaged in a terrific struggle. One got the other down and killed him, bundling the body through the door into the cave beyond. He then buried the knife with which the deed was done, though curiously enough this detail was only observed by the husband, who actually unearthed a knife afterwards at the spot. Both witnesses then saw the murderer pass them, and they followed him into the dining-room, where he drank some brandy, though this action was seen by the wife and not the husband. He then took off his boots, exactly as the nurse had already described. With his boots in his hand he ascended the stairs and passed through the panel as he had done so often before, the inference being that on each previous occasion the scene in the cellar had preceded his advent.

Inquiry now showed that many years ago the house had been inhabited by two brothers who amassed considerable wealth by smuggling. They had hoarded their money in partnership, but one of them finally announced his intention of getting married, which involved his drawing his share of the treasure. Soon afterwards this brother disappeared, and it was rumoured that he had gone to sea upon a long voyage. So far as I remember, for I write with only notes of the episode before me, the other brother went mad, and the affair was never cleared up in his lifetime. It should be added that the panel into which the vision disappeared concealed a large cupboard, which might well have been the treasure-house of the establishment. The graphic touch of the boots carried in the hand suggests that there was some housekeeper or other resident who might be disturbed by the sound of the murderer's footsteps.

In this case one can certainly imagine that in so fratricidal a strife there would be a peculiar intensity of emotion on the part of both the actors, which would leave a marked record if anything could do so.

That the record was indeed very marked is shown by the fact that the sight was not reserved for people with psychic qualities, like the first two instances here recorded, but that everyone, the husband, the wife, and the nurse all saw the apparition, which must therefore have been particularly solid even after the lapse of so many years. It might, I think, be put forward as a hypothesis supplementary to that of thoughtforms thrown off in times of crisis, that the permanency and solidity of the form depend upon the extremity of the emotion.

A second illustration may be drawn from Mrs. Tweedale's reminiscences. I am taking my cases from a limited number of books, for the sake of convenience in reference, but they are typical of very many others. The most absurd of the many absurd charges against Spiritualism is that it has no literature. It has actually a literature with which no other religion could attempt to compare, and it may safely be said that if an assiduous reader were to devour nothing else for fifty years he would be very far from having got to the end of it. Its quality is not on a par with its quantity, but even there I would undertake to name fifty books on the scientific and religious sides of Spiritualism which would outweigh in interest, dignity, and brain-power an equal list from any other philosophy. Yet the public is kept absolutely ignorant of the greater part of these remarkable works, many of which will one day be world-famous. The people who acted and wrote in the Apostolic epoch of the Christian Church little thought how their actions would appear two thousand years later, and certainly the supercilious philosophers and scandalized high priests would have been much astounded to know of the changed values which time has created.

To return, however, to the further illustration, it concerns the doings in a shooting-lodge in Argyllshire, inhabited in 1901 by Major and Mrs. Stewart, the latter being the sister of Mrs. Tweedale. The starting-point of this haunting had been a situation which would form a grim theme for a novelist. An elderly farmer, who was a widower with a grown-up son, married a young girl. His son soon learned to love his stepmother, and the love may have been passionately returned. The result was a struggle in which the son was killed by the father. It is not to be wondered at that so horrible an event should leave a great psychic disturbance behind it, and the lodge was found to be a storm-centre of the unknown forces. The phenomena, which seem to have occurred every night, took the form of loud thuds and crashes, especially in a certain room upon the upper floor, which had probably been a bedroom. Footsteps resounded down the stairs, and upon one occasion the whole terrible fight was enacted in the passage, with all the blows and curses of the infuriated men. The tragedy may well have commenced upstairs, the guilty son have fled to the door, and been overtaken by his father in the hall below. The impressions seem to have been entirely auditory, though a clairvoyant would no doubt have seen the scene even as it occurred. This case closely resembles the last, in that the most furious human passions must have been aroused, so that every condition existed for a permanent psychic record. It should be added that in this latter instance four Pomeranian dogs in the house were reduced to abject terror, showing that there was no hallucination upon the part of the human observers.

In discussing reasons for these and similar phenomena we must not make the mistake of supposing that one single explanation can cover all the range of the facts. To do so would be to court disaster, for someone could at once produce a case which could not be so covered. These instances which have been quoted have all sprung from scenes of emotion, and all represent, as I venture to suggest, mere shadow-forms detached from the real personality. There is another class of case, however, which produces much the same result, since haunting forms are seen, but which differs utterly in its nature, in that the forms appear to be the actual materialized spirits of the dead held fast by their thoughts and desires to some spot which they have loved upon earth. Such a bondage would probably seem by no means unpleasant to them, and might only mean that in the interval of such duties as they might find awaiting them in a new life they loved to return to the old happy scene of their earth-memories. Thus, Brother John, in *The Gate of Remembrance*, was an entirely good and happy spirit, and no doubt had its duties elsewhere, yet his great love for Glastonbury Abbey brought him down whenever the interests of the old ruins demanded it. All accounts of the wandering of dead misers and others round the scene of their earthly ambitions would probably come in a lower and less happy degree under the same head. One excellent and typical example of what I mean was the case of the old Kent manor-house as detailed by Mr. Dale Owen.

The narrative concerns Ramhurst Manor House, near Leigh, in Kent, and was compiled in 1857. The house was inhabited by the family of a British general, who were much disturbed by noises at night and other happenings. A clairvoyante young lady, who came as a visitor, was able to give them some information, her experience bearing out the rule already stated, that psychic hearing is easier and more common than psychic sight. She could see where the others could only hear. The ghosts who presented themselves were an elderly couple, dressed as in a bygone age, who actually stood upon the threshold to welcome her. After meeting them several times they spoke to her, and this marks a difference from all the shadow-forms already described, none of which show any sign of individual thought and speech. These old people explained that they had once lived in the Manor House, and that their name on earth was Children. They declared that they had idolized their property, that its improvement was the centre of their thoughts, and that they were now grieved to see that it had passed away to strangers. It was a case where total absorption in an earthly thing, however innocent, had become a fatal bar to spiritual advancement—a danger against which we must all earnestly guard. Their voices as they spoke seemed normal to the young lady, while the point lace upon the beautifully-brocaded dress was imprinted in her memory. The living lady of the house was able soon afterwards to confirm the statement of her clairvoyante friend, for she also saw the female vision with the name, "Dame Children," written above her in letters of phosphoric fire, together with a statement that she was "earth-bound." For some time diligent inquiry could not find any trace of a family of this unusual name having ever occupied the house, but finally a very old woman was found who in her youth had met an aged man who said that in his boyhood he had helped in the kennels of the Children family. Mr. Dale Owen was so interested in the case that he personally investigated it and cross-examined all the witnesses. On asking the young lady whether the ghost had said anything else of an evidential nature, she remembered that Richard was given as the name of the man, and that the date 1753 was associated with his death. Following up his researches, Mr. Dale Owen discovered some account of the Manor House, which concluded with the words: "Richard Children, Esqre., resided here and died possessed of it in 1753, aged eighty-three years. He was succeeded in it by . . . George Children who is the present possessor."

This narrative must carry conviction with it to any reasonable mind, though I must refer the reader to Dale Owen's *Footfalls* for the smaller details which mean so much. It suggests that the whole range of hauntings of this nature spring from undue preoccupation and want of spiritual effort. One such case seems to carry more warning than all the sermons that ever were spoken. At the same time, Providence is not cruel, and, as I have said, the bondage which is formed by earth-thoughts need not really be an unhappy one to those who are held by it.

When separated into the mere shadows or thought-forms on one side, and actual earth-bound spirits on the other, it is not difficult to analyse and understand a large proportion of preternatural happenings. The division is admittedly a temporary hypothesis, but it serves to keep some sort of order in a subject which has until recently been a mad chaos of inexplicable effects without rational cause. Cases will still obtrude themselves, however, which disturb the tidiness of the most well-ordered theories, and I do not know a more baffling one than that which is treated by two English school-mistresses, and admirably described in their little book called *An Adventure*.

This adventure, shortly told, consisted in the fact that during a visit to Paris they entered the gardens of Versailles in order to see the Grand Trianon, and that while in those gardens they had a most extraordinary experience, which in the case of one of the ladies was repeated with variations upon the occasion of a second visit. They suddenly appeared to be in the gardens as they were a century before, at the time of the French Revolution, and to see, and in some cases actually speak with, gardeners, messengers, and others who were there in the days of Marie Antoinette. So natural was it all, beginning and ending with normal life, that the ladies hardly understood what had happened to them until they began to compare notes, and realized that some of the buildings and garden arrangements which they had seen had not existed within the memory of man. Both ladies carried away a clear remembrance of dignified officials in grey-green coats and small three-cornered hats, of an intensely still landscape, of trees that looked like tapestry, of cloaked, large-hatted figures, of a running messenger who shouted instructions to them, of a long-waisted, full-skirted lady with a pale-green fichu, of a jaunty young footman, and other quite definite details—all this at four o'clock of a summer afternoon. A second visit by one lady alone, some four months later, produced similar effects, differing in detail but not in general character from the first.

Such an experience is so very unlike the vast majority of psychic cases that one is inclined to push it aside. If one cannot get a document into a pigeon-hole, one is too ready with a wastepaper basket, and it is this human tendency which has retarded our advance in this new science. Anyone who carefully reads the narrative of these ladies, and notices the points of resemblance and also the very interesting points of divergence in their stories, cannot fail to take them seriously. It was not imagination or suggestion or, so far as one can judge, hallucination. But what it was, and why by some strange psychic refraction this mirage of the past should be thrown down upon the present, is an insoluble problem. It must at least teach us that, however much our tiny brains may endeavour to comprehend and classify these extraordinary phenomena, there still remain so many unknown causes and unexplained conditions that for many a long year to come our best efforts can only be regarded as well-meant approximations to the truth.

III
NOTES FROM
A STRANGE MAIL-BAG

THE DREAMERS

FOR MANY YEARS I have been the recipient of as strange a shower of letters as one could imagine. They come from all sorts of folk who have had all sorts of psychic experiences. They demand sympathy, advice and explanation. The former I can give, but the latter are not always so easy. The handling of this correspondence has added a burden to my already over-weighted days, but it is not work which I can hand to a delegate, since very often fine points of knowledge are involved, and the letters are exceedingly confidential and personal. I am glad to think that I have left few unanswered, but it has been at the expense of much energy and time which might, perhaps, have been better employed in some more general fashion. And yet some good end might be attained if I could use them discreetly in order to ventilate in public the various matters discussed.

If the reader likes to treat the cases as instances of delusion or of peculiar mental aberration that is for his own judgment to decide. I only put forward the letters as being very real facts to those who wrote them. The rest is a matter of individual opinion. From my cabinet of tabulated drawers I take down the one which is labelled "Dreams," and I pick a few of the contents almost at haphazard.

Here is a very vivid letter from a lady who is herself a musical composer. She dreamed that she was in the presence of a great celestial choir. Her account is an arresting one, and none can doubt that some tremendous impact had been made upon her mind.

"The orchestra was of vast size—something like the seating capacity of the Albert Hall. The conductor and the singers were on my right, but after they started playing I realized that they were all round me, and there was a great bank of strings on my left. They were playing what seemed like the end of a classical symphony and the speed they took it at far exceeded any tempo I've heard here. It was like a sea of bows flashing up and down. As I watched them a curious thing happened. It seemed as if the senses of sight and sound merged into one faculty, and that I could see the vibrations from those violins. You remember the spray mist which hangs over Niagara Falls. Just such a shimmering haze seemed to float above the players. The other thing that struck me was the ideal beauty of the ensemble. That mighty host of players were like one thought and action. It so far exceeded anything I have heard here as to be almost overpowering. My own sense of perfection could hardly stretch to it. It was marvellous. Of course, my thoughts are continually on music and rehearsals, so that itself would not convey much, but this idea of seeing sound vibrations never entered my conscious thoughts, and that is the most vivid impression of the dream."

Though the lady did not know it, the idea of the close connection between colour and sound is one which has frequently come to us in what purported to be descriptions of life in the Beyond. I could very readily find a dozen illustrations of the fact among those posthumous accounts which profess to describe the experiences which await us. The general idea of concerted music is also very familiar. "I play in an orchestra and I enjoy it so much." Such was a message which I received myself recently from a friend who was fond of music. Lester Coltman the Guardsman, in what is asserted to be his after-death experience, says:

"Orchestration is my great hobby here," and adds: "For some time after I passed over I was undecided as to whether music or science should be my work. After much serious thought, I determined that music should be my hobby and my more earnest intent should be directed upon science in every form."

It may be said generally that the evidence of psychic research agrees with the vague Christian tradition that music plays a large part in the higher spheres.

The next letter which I pick up deals with a very much less elevated impression. This is an American writing from San José, California, who dreams names.

"If I can identify the name with some race-horse, I have found that the horse has, nine times out of ten, won the race. I am not interested in horse-racing, and have not been on a track for twenty years."

The next letter is also about horse-racing, from a retired Captain in Ireland. In his case he claims to get a picture, not a name. He is not a betting man and makes no use of his information, which is just as well for the bookies. Going over his results, I find that he seldom got a winner, but that his horses were invariably placed. It was a curious dumb-crambo system of conveying names, when supplied by vision, but occasionally they came in an audible voice at the moment of waking from sleep. What are we to make of such an experience? Is it imagination followed by coincidence? Or is it of some humble psychic origin? We have to place on the other side the many cases where such dreams have betrayed us. Only last year I had the experience of backing the dream of a friend for the Derby, and being five pounds poorer as a consequence.

The next letter takes us back into the black days of the War. It is from an English lady living in Finland. Her younger brother was killed at the front in one of the final battles in a dawn attack. At that hour the lady went through his whole experience, visualized the battlefield, heard the guns, and saw an elderly and moustached German who threw something—presumably a bomb—which struck her down. Some nights later she had a second equally vivid dream in which a radiant spirit led her along a poplar-lined French road and halted at last at the spot where the dead body of her brother was lying. She declares that she had every reason at the time to think that her brother was at a depot and not in the firing-line. It was after the Armistice that official news was given of his death. This is one of a class of cases which has been so common that no reasonable man can deny them. To explain them is another matter, for even if one accepts the full faith of Spiritualism there is a good deal which is inexplicable.

The next item is from the West of America. The writer has three times during ten years had an extraordinary and very vivid dream which has always been the same. He was in each case commanding the bodyguard of an Oriental Sultan and had to defend a palace attacked by rebels. On each occasion he was killed and found himself after death looking down upon a litter of dead bodies. The country in which these incidents occurred gradually revealed itself to him as being Oman upon the east coast of Arabia, and the dreamer actually opened a correspondence with the Sultan of Muscat, a letter from whom he enclosed to me as a proof of good faith. The Sultan took a lively interest in the matter and was anxious that the dreamer should visit him, but the coming of the War intervened. The American protests that he is still planning to go to Muscat, though one would have thought that it is the one place which he would have carefully avoided. No sequel has yet been reported, though the letter is two years old.

I pick up a letter now which is of a most interesting type. It is from a lady in Chicago. She lay at the point of death with a temperature of 105°. She was insensible but dreaming vividly. She seemed to hear music of unearthly beauty, and to be surrounded by the faces of many loved ones who had passed on. The only sensation was one of delicious languor.

"It was the most vivid and beautiful dream I ever experienced. When I came to myself I thought that if death was like that I should not mind going at any time. Is it then possible for the soul to leave the body for a short while and then to return again?"

My answer was that I had numerous similar cases which seemed to show that it *was* possible, and that such knowledge did indeed remove all fear of death.

The next letter is also from an American lady and is not very dissimilar in its subject. It was not the weakness of disease but it was the emotion produced by music which, in her case, seems to have effected a

66

temporary dissociation between soul and body. The opera was "Manon Lescaut" and Caruso the singer.

"At the grand climax," she writes, "I seemed to float away upward, quite overwhelmed. After the curtain fell I was still away. The live part of me had separated from my body and it was with the greatest difficulty that I forced myself together. With a look of consternation the lady next me observed my condition."

Reduced to common speech all this simply means that the lady was on the point of fainting, and yet it may make us ask ourselves what we mean exactly when we use the phrase.

The dream which duplicates an actual occurrence is hard to explain, but an even tougher problem is presented by the prophetic dream which gives a picture of the future. My next letter is from a man in Liverpool who found himself in his sleep standing by a railway station and looking up a sloping road with another road at right angles at the top. There was a bridge above him, and over the bridge came a tramcar on which was painted some strange place names of which he had never heard. Some months later he visited Wrexham for the first time and there he found the station, the road, the slope, the bridge and the tram, which had Welsh names on the outside. Nothing arose from the incident, and there seemed no possible reason why it should have been shot into the sleeper's mind months beforehand. In the case of this and similar incidents which are both trivial and psychic, one can only suppose that an attempt is made—we cannot say by whom—to awaken the interest of the recipient in spiritual matters by showing him things which are outside the ken of material science. It certainly has such an effect, for the man who has had such an experience is far more open afterwards to psychic knowledge. An alternative explanation would be that in one of those nocturnal rambles which our souls or etheric bodies do seem to take, the dreamer visited Wrexham—possibly drawn by the fact that he had relatives living there—and that he chanced to carry back some memory of its appearance. The tram might well be running in the early morning.

A second experience by the same gentleman rather supports the latter explanation. He dreamed that he saw a lady friend working at some pink material. On inquiry she said, "Yes, I stayed up late last night making a crêpe de Chine blouse of pink stuff, which I particularly wished to finish." Since she was late it is probable that his dream saw that which was actually occurring at the moment, and that it was an instance of what has been called "travelling clairvoyance" where the etheric body brings back information—surprisingly trivial information at times—to the unconscious material brain.

The next item is less complex. It comes from Battersea. A Mrs. Arbuthnot dreamed that her life was threatened by a friend whom we will call Mrs. Burton. When she told the dream she was not aware that Mrs. Burton had at that time a maniacal attack in which she imagined she had some deadly grievance against her friend. This would appear to be a clear case of telepathy. I may add that telepathy, which is constantly given as an explanation of other psychic happenings, is, in my opinion, among the less common phenomena, and is by no means so clearly established as some of the physical manifestations.

To return to prophetic dreams: they are occasionally of a very helpful character, as the next example will show. The writer is a Manchester man fresh from Cambridge. During a visit to Switzerland he dreamed that he was in a tropical land, sandy, with a shimmering heat and an intensely blue sky. Suddenly, a huge man appeared before him holding a triangular dagger of peculiar shape, with which he made the motion of striking. He then vanished. Next day the youth explored a disused tunnel.

"I went in and found magnificent icicles hanging from the roof. All at once I saw one very large one. It was triangular and came to a sharp point. I thought of my dream, and recognized the triangular dagger. I stopped, and at that moment the whole thing fell with a crash. It must have weighed at least two hundred pounds and would perhaps have killed me."

What are we to make of this? Is it not beyond coincidence? And how are we to explain the tropical scene? I would only suggest—but with all reserve—that many of us believe that we have guides or guardian angels. These guides would appear to be often drawn from the Oriental races. Supposing that this youth's guide was an Egyptian; he might, in warning his pupil, have brought back with him some impression of his native land. The student remarked that the dagger was of a shape which was once used in Ancient Egypt. Such an explanation may stand until a better one is found.

A number of these dreams are concerned with objects which have been lost and found again by revelation. There is always the consideration that such finds may have been the result of some subconscious train of thought, as occurs so often in our everyday experience, when the solution of some problem wells suddenly up from the unknown depths of our mentality. But in some cases this would seem to be impossible. Here, for example, is a letter from Bath. The writer was a solicitor in a South African city. He had a client to whose father in early days a grant of land had been made on the outskirts of the city. At the time it was of no value, but as the city spread it became so, but very many years had passed and the grant was lost. One night the client dreamed where it was. Next day, accompanied by a resident who knew the town well, he walked to the place of his dream, identified a certain cottage, had his knock answered by a lady whom he had seen in his sleep, walked through to an outhouse, opened an old box and plucked out the grant which had been stuffed into an envelope tacked to the inside of the lid. It is sad to relate that after all this trouble the grant was not admitted by the new generation of officials. But the story told as it is by the solicitor concerned, seems to be incontrovertible. What are we to make of it? Here, again, we seem to be balanced between the possibilities of the wandering soul and those of external intelligence. In any case, such incidents deserve our best consideration, and our men of Science may well turn their minds from the insects and the stones in order to unravel problems so intimately related to our own nature and fate.

The next letter happens to be from the same quarter and on a similar subject. It tells the tale of a *Muizenberg* lady who lost her box and had successive dreams of it for several months during its various and devious wanderings, until she at last saw it in her sleep reposing upon the shelf of the lost property office, whence she duly reclaimed it next morning. When one reads such an account one feels a certain sense of injury as we survey our own losses, and we wonder why we also should not all have such help. Here we must admit that we are on the edge of the unknown. The wireless message comes sharp and clear when we tune in to the exact vibration. A fraction above or below and it is gone. Here, too, there may be unconscious tuning-in of the receiver. But what is the transmitter? That is the next great problem which faces humanity.

It is clear that to find the right receiver is difficult, otherwise messages would not be sent in so indirect a fashion. The next example illustrates what I mean. A London lady gets a message, or rather a vision, which assures her that an unknown woman, who is embracing two children, is about to "go on her last journey—her last, long, strange journey." The actual message and the name, Mrs. Lorimer, came audibly. On inquiry the dreamer found that there was such a woman, that she had two children, and subsequently that she died. We may well deduce that if the receptive power were a common one the message would certainly have been given more directly and not in a way which was so distant that it might well have miscarried.

I have spoken of the night travels of the etheric body. I come now to a very remarkable example of it—unique, so far as I know, because the return to the material body was slow and clearly remembered. The gentleman who writes to me—a Manchester man—fell asleep before his fire. He woke up still seated in a chair in the early morning and glanced at the clock. It marked 12:15 but—it was not *his* clock.

With amazed eyes he looked along the mantelpiece. Everything was strange. There were two big bronzes of equestrian figures. The mantelpiece itself was of heavy red marble. The fire-irons were of massive brass. He was so petrified that it was a long time before he could bring himself to look round. When at last he cautiously turned his head he found himself in a very large room lined with books. There was a reading-lamp on a long central table, and a man was seated at it. My correspondent was filled with the idea that he had wandered into some stranger's house, so with an effort he rose and addressed the man at the table. Getting no answer he touched him. As the man took no notice and remained very still the writer was speculating whether he was dead, when he suddenly turned the pages and went on reading. At this instant the walls of the room seemed to whirl round and my correspondent found himself in his own chair, facing his own clock, and with the time registered at 12:25. He winds up his narrative with the words, "I give you my most solemn word of honour that I have told you what I consider to be the truth."

Accepting this final statement we have to find a rational explanation. The most rational surely is that the process of travelling clairvoyance and the return from the dream journey were done slowly and consciously, instead of coming in a flash. Had the latter been the case the dreamer would simply have had a vague recollection of some large room with books in it, and it would in no way have differed from a normal dream impression. But, for some reason, the process was carried out slowly and in stages. The etheric body came to conscious life—a life which could be registered on the material brain—while making itself very comfortable in front of the fire of what would appear to have been a Club library with one belated member therein. The insubstantial etheric body was unable to impress the material senses of the reader, but it is possible that if the latter had looked up from his book he might have had a wonderful ghost story to tell for the rest of his life. Then came the belated return, when, like a homing pigeon, the wandering soul shoots swiftly and unerringly back to its body. Should it lose its way, then one more mortal has died in his sleep.

There is some evidence that it is more easy for these dream messages to be conveyed to us by pictures and symbols than by words, though sometimes the picture comes first and then the explanatory message. At the time, early in the War, when there was alarm about the fate of Maurice Hewlett's son, a lady in Scotland had a clear vision of a man being rescued from a seaplane, and an audible message came, "That is Maurice Hewlett's son. He is rescued." This was put on record at the time; a fact which I have tested, for I have before me a document.

"We, the undersigned, declare that the account of this dream was given to us, as written, before the announcement of the rescue appeared."

This is signed by two witnesses. One could hardly wish for a clearer case than this, but it may have been the travelling soul of the dreamer which carried back both the picture and the message. Again, I have an account from a French lady whose husband managed the household affairs in an unsatisfactory way. She saw her dead father, who handed her a large key. This key opened a door which led to a room which was exceedingly untidy, but became all right again when the lady entered. She took the dream to mean that she was to be mistress in her own house, and acted accordingly, with the best results. Here the appearance of the father certainly gives an other-world flavour to the transaction.

Such dreams are useful, but occasionally I read of one which is so

71

useless that one is hard put to it when one tries to weave it into any philosophy. Thus one correspondent dreamed that a child was born to him, which was so discoloured in the body that it would appear to have been scorched. A policeman was mixed up with the dream. Next morning a policeman entered his shop with a summons to a jury for an inquest. The case proved to be that of a poor tramp who had been badly scorched by his straw bed taking fire. Such an incident is not entirely beyond coincidence, and in no case does it seem to have served any purpose.

Sometimes one can see no object in the communication, and yet the psychic evidence is very strong and is calculated to turn the mind of the recipient to spiritual interpretations of life. Thus in the case of a Mrs. Lofty, she writes to say that she lost her son, Grantham Lofty, in a flying mishap.

"One day I felt like ending everything, when it was suggested to me in the most clear way that I should think of my dream."

It seems that two years before the lady and a friend had both dreamed the same dream on the same night. The dream included a message that James Lofty was dying or dead in No. 7 Ward.

"I wrote out the dream at once and sent it to my sister."

Immediately after the tragedy occurred, two years after the dream, the lady visited Haslar Hospital, and found that the ward in which her son died was No. 7, and that by some error his name on the hospital books had been entered as James. This certainly is a complex and remarkable case, but it seems to have assured the mother of his continued existence and consoled her in the hour of need.

One very common dream impression which may well be connected with those soul wanderings which come, in my opinion, well within the category of things proven, is the feeling of flying. It often occurs to dreamers, but more to some than to others in proportion as their switch-off is absolute or partial. Thus a dreamer writes from South Carolina.

"One dream comes to me over and over again. At least one thousand times I have dreamed that I was exercising a power transporting my body through the air in defiance of gravitation. Usually I just lift my feet from the ground and will myself to float in the desired direction without any physical effort. At other times, when I wish to reach a higher level, I work my arms as if they were wings. I seem in my dreams to call the attention of ordinary mortals to what I am doing, but if they possess the power to see it they never make any comment on it."

They would, of course, no more see it than the man in the Club library saw the etheric body which touched him on the shoulder.

Several of these letters—and perhaps the most important—allude to the perceptions which the dreamers carry back of some wonderful land which some of us think is actually the etheric world, suited for etheric life, and which others may try to explain as a glimpse of our own tropics, or as some imaginative scene which has no actual existence. It is as real to the dreamer, as was that clock in the Club library upon which the sleeper read the time, and equally real seem those figures with whom they hold converse.

Here is the sort of thing from a correspondent:

"I have twice in sleep crossed over into the spirit world. The radiance and wonderful beauty of the country was what struck me more than anything. I felt, above all, that this was a land of extraordinary happiness. On the first occasion I met and spoke with my brother. On the second I saw no one, but was deeply impressed by the beauty of the lake and hills among which I found myself. The colours were indeed different from those on earth. They had an exceeding glory."

This matches very closely a large number of other descriptions. I am aware of all the difficulties connected with such a view of the Beyond. We are faced with the obvious reflection that hills and valleys are the result of geological action, of rain and age-long denudation, so that their existence, from our point of view, would seem to imply similar actions in their formation. It is a legitimate and cogent objection. And yet, the positive agreement of a great number of witnesses cannot be easily set aside. Some have thought that this old earth may have its own etheric body, even as its inhabitants have. Certainly, if we are to cut out all effects of earthly elemental action, heaven would become a flat and waterless expanse, which would seem more logical than attractive.

In discussing dream appearances of the other spheres, I may perhaps be permitted to give an experience of my own—though I may quote with all reverence, "Whether in the body or out of it, I know not." I had been told at a séance that I should visit in my sleep some other sphere, upon which I earnestly begged that I might carry back the memory. There followed an eventful night, some of which is quite as clear to me as any adventure I have had upon the earth's surface.

My first impression was that of a row of rather dilapidated stone villas, such as one would see in the suburbs of Edinburgh. They looked well in front but were only half-finished within, though I observed pictures upon the walls—frescoes rather, since they seemed to be part of the wall. There was waste ground around, untidy and weed-covered. I saw no dwellers in these uncomfortable buildings, but I was aware all through that I had a companion at my side, whose face I never saw. This invisibility did not seem to worry me at the time, and I made no attempt to get past it.

Then, with no consciousness of an intervening journey, I was in another place. It was a large hall or assembly place. Once again there were coloured frescoes on the wall, but I carried away no impression of the subjects. There were pillars and an ornamental ceiling. Close to me was standing a man dressed in Elizabethan dress. He had a plum-coloured doublet and trunk hose. We eyed each other and I was so completely myself that I smiled and said, "Well, if you fellows are going to dress like that we poor moderns have no chance." He made no answer, and his face was quite unresponsive. I could recognize the man now if I saw him, ruddy-faced, about thirty-five years of age, short, crisp, black hair and a black moustache, well-built and vigorous. He was sullen and sinister in his expression. I was conscious of someone else approaching with a black Spanish cloak. Then it all disappeared.

I was not in a vehicle of some sort—I have no impression of a horse, but I was more conscious than before of my companion. There was a vague feeling of hurry—we had to be at a certain place by a certain time. The road was broad and curving, with a hill-side upon the left with some ancient ruins built right into it. At the top of the hill we stopped. A wonderful panorama of a city lay before me. It was built upon low hills and it undulated away to the horizon. The sky and atmosphere were grey, but not more so than London on a winter day. I

74

have never seen so great a city. High buildings and towers stretched as far as I could see, but I saw no spires. Then all faded away, and I awoke.

It was a very intense experience and I give the explanation which I received next day from psychic sources for what the reader may think it is worth. It came in reply to questions.

"It was a probationary city. Those pictures were instructive to people in that stage. You did not see your guide because it would have taken from the power. The power was running low, so we had to hurry in the end. You were taken to a grey city because that side of spirit life has always excited your sympathy and curiosity."

Such was my most vivid nocturnal experience.

Dreaming true is the only psychic power which I have hitherto developed outside healing. Before we went to Australia I got the name "Naldern" imprinted on my mind in sleep and wrote it down on waking. We sailed in the "Naldera," though we had intended another ship and had never consciously heard of the former. Again, I have put it on record before the event how I dreamed that the Piave would be the turning-point of the War, many months before the Italians were driven back sixty miles to that position, where they won their decisive victory. In literature I have had little help from dreams. Once I woke with a line ringing in my head. It was, "She walked alone on the Hills of Fate." I wrote a poem called "Victrix" round it, and it marks my highest point, perhaps, on the foothills of Parnassus.

I may conclude these notes by stating my opinion as to the exact nature of dreams, as I have already done in my *New Revelation*. There seem to me to be two forms, and only two: one, the experiences of the released spirit, and the other, the confused action of the lower faculties which remain in the body when the spirit is absent. The former is rare and beautiful, but the memory of it fails us. The latter is common and varied, but usually fantastic or ignoble. By noting what is absent in the lower dreams one can tell what the missing qualities are, and so judge what part of us goes to make up the spirit. Thus in these dreams humour is wanting, since we see things which strike us afterwards as ludicrous, and are not amused. The sense of proportion and of judgment are all gone. In short, the higher is palpably gone, and the lower, the sense of fear, of sensual impression, of self-preservation, are functioning all the more vividly because they are relieved from the higher control.

IV

THE GHOST OF THE MOAT

IF ANYONE CRAVES for adventure, he will find it in psychic work. I have myself encountered many incidents in actual fact which I could hardly beat if I gave free play to my imagination.

Some mention of Dr. and Mrs. Wickland of Los Angeles have occasionally found their way into the Press. He is a deep student of psychic phenomena believing, as I do myself, that a great deal of mania and crime is due to direct obsession, and that a recognition of the fact would be the first necessary step for dealing with it.

She is a medium who is very sensitive to spirit presences, and is ready, with great bravery, to allow them to control her so long as she thinks a good purpose can be served. She is, in my opinion, one of the heroines of the world. Such were the couple, gentle, elderly folk, who drove out with us to see something of rural Sussex.

I took them to the old moated grange of Groombridge, which is mentioned by Evelyn in his Diary. As we stood looking at the lichened brick walls, a door which gave upon the deep moat opened and a woman looked out. Then it closed again. We passed on, and I thought no more of the matter.

As we walked through the meadow which led to the high road Mrs. Wickland kept glancing back. Presently she said:

"There is such a strange old man walking beside us."

"What is he like?"

"He is old. His face is sunk forward. His back is hunched. He is earth-bound."

"How is he dressed?"

"He has knee-breeches, a striped vest, and quite a short coat."

"Whence did he come?"

"He came through that door that opened."

"Then how did he cross the moat?"

"I don't know, and I don't know what he wants, but he is at our heels."

I took my guests to the old Crown Inn in the village, where we had tea. Mrs. Wickland kept glancing at a chair in the corner beside her.

"He is there." Presently she began to laugh.

"I did not in the least want that second cup of tea, and the extra slice," she said, "but he was close to me, and would have taken possession and helped himself if I had not done so."

We had driven home, and were seated among the roses on my veranda, the Wicklands, my wife, and myself. We were talking of other things when the Seer suddenly gave a start.

"He's here."

Then came the amazing moment. Before our eyes she changed in an instant into a heavy-faced, sullen old man, with bent back and loose, senile lips. The whole expression was utterly different. She choked and spluttered in an effort to express the thoughts of the control.

Dr. Wickland, with the quiet assurance of long practice, massaged the throat.

"All right, friend, give yourself time."

The new-comer shook off his hand angrily.

"Leave me alone. What do you want to touch me for?" he croaked.

From that time the dialogue was as follows, sometimes one and sometimes another asking the questions, and with occasional gaspings and chokings as interruption.

"Who are you?"

"I am from Groombridge. My name? Well, I don't feel clear in my mind. Yes, yes, I remember. It is David. And Fletcher. That is it, David Fletcher. Yes, I have been in service there. Horses. Yes, it was the horses I looked to. What year is it? I don't know. My mind ain't clear. Is it 1808 or is it 1809? What d'ye say, 1927? Well, well, that's a good 'un."

78

"Dead, why, I am here talkin' to you. How can I be dead? I'd be with God if I was dead." (Suddenly started.) "Look at my hand? Why there are rings on it. They look like my lady's rings. No, I don't know how they came to be there."

"I don't understand a lot of things. I don't know who them folk are in the house. They have no call to be there. Me and the others try to put them out." ("The others," Dr. Wickland explained, "were probably other earth-bound spirits in the old house.")

"Yes, master was a good master, but he died, and the others came in. The house was sold. We wasn't well treated after that. What could I do? No, I couldn't go away. Where was I to go out in the wide world, and me with a hump on my back? I belonged to the house. I had to do the best I could."

"What have I done? I don't rightly understand it. I've slept always in the same old corner. It seems a long, long time."

"Now tell us, David, don't you remember being very ill?"

"Me ill? No, I was never ill. But I'll tell you what happened. He pushed me into the water."

"Into the moat?"

"Yes, into the water."

"Who was he?"

"It was Sam." (Many chuckles.) "But I held on to him, I did. He came in the water, too." (Dr. Wickland remarked that the man was probably drowned on that occasion.)

"Is there no one who loved you among the dead? Was your mother dead?"

"Mother was dead. No one ever loved me, except mother. She loved me, mother did. No one could love me, because I looked queer. They laughed." (He burst into noisy sobbing.) "Mother loved me. Nobody else. They said it wasn't right that I wait upon the ladies, and me with a hump."

"Cheer up, David; we will soon get the hump off you. How came you to follow us?"

"I don't know. I think I was told. Then I got bread and tea. I have not had tea since I can remember. I would like more. I am always hungry. But what was that wagon? That was the devil's wagon, I think. I got in, but it went that fast that I was afeared to get out again." (This was my motor.)

"It's as well for you that you did not, for we are going to do you good, David. First of all you have got to realize that you are dead. You were drowned that time you fell into the moat."

"Well I never. That's a queer idea."

"Now understand this." (It is Dr. Wickland, who is talking in cool, gentle, assured tones.) "You can do anything now by the power of thought, if you know how to use it. This hump of yours. Take it off. Take it off, I say. Your back is as straight as mine." (The bent figure began to straighten up and to sit erect in the chair. Suddenly both hands were thrown forward.)

"Mother, mother." (His face had become younger, more intelligent and was shining with ecstasy.) "I see her and it's mother, but she looks younger than I can remember."

"She will take charge of you now. You have been brought here by higher powers for a purpose—to save you. Do you want to go back to the old house?"

"No, no, I want to go to mother. Oh you good kind people"—the rest was just incoherent gratitude.

And so it was that the earth-bound ostler found his mother at last among the rambler roses of my balcony. Have I not said truly that the actual experiences of the Spiritualist, of which this is one in a hundred, are stranger far than what I should dare to invent?

Is it all a fairy-tale? How about the change in the medium? How about the ostler's dress so accurately described? How about the cases where the actual names and addresses have been verified by the Wicklands?

It is not a fairy-tale, but it is a new realm of knowledge which the human race has now to explore and conquer.

V

THE LAW OF THE GHOST

IT IS SAFE to say that for some centuries to come the human race will be very actively engaged in defining the laws which regulate psychic affairs, and it is fortunately a line of study which has the peculiar advantage to those who indulge in it that they can pursue it just as well, and probably better, from the other side of the veil. At present there is work lying to hand for a hundred investigators. The innumerable records which exist in various forms, and which are scattered throughout papers, magazines, reports of learned societies, family traditions, etc., are like masses of ore which have been extracted from the ground but are still lying in dumps waiting to be separated into precious ingots on the one side and slag-heap on the other. They have to be examined, collected into classes, reviewed in the light of our ever-increasing psychic knowledge, and an endeavour made to find underlying principles running through this vague collection of matter, so that at last we may touch solid ground by getting hold of some elementary laws. The first thing is that we should have authentic cases so that the foundation of our reasoning may be sound. The second is to compare these authentic cases together and see what common characteristics they possess, shirking nothing and following the facts wherever they lead without any preliminary prejudice. This is, of course, the true scientific fashion, but it is unfortunately one which has been neglected by most scientific men in approaching this new subject which would not fit in with their preconceived ideas. Let us hunt among these fascinating problems for shards and splinters out of which a noble mosaic will one day be constructed, and let us see whether here and there we may not find two or three pieces which fit together, and give some idea of a permanent pattern, even though it be a fantastic one. I will begin by telling three stories which seem to be absolutely authentic, and then we shall endeavour to trace some underlying connection.

For full particulars of the first case the reader is referred to *West Indian Tales*, by Algernon Aspinall, with the explanation that the word "Tales" is not used in the sense of inventions, and that the facts are authentic, as is proved by numerous references in the narrative. These facts relate to the singular series of events which happened in connection with the vault at Christ-church, near the village of Oistin, on the south coast of Barbados. In the old slave days when rum and sugar were the foundations of many a goodly fortune, things were done on a large scale in the West Indies, and this burial vault was a very fine one. It was made of great blocks of coral and cement, partly sunk into the earth, for the graveyard was on an exposed hill, and terrific storms sweep over these latitudes. The entrance was covered by a huge slab of marble. Within, the dimensions of the vault were twelve feet by six and a half. So Cyclopean was the masonry and so remote the site that one would imagine an inmate was almost as secure as a king of Egypt in the heart of his pyramid. A contractor and a gang of skilled workmen would be needed to effect an entrance into so solid a construction. Little did those who erected it imagine that the whole island would be convulsed by the repeated proofs of its insecurity.

In July, 1807, a Mrs. Goddard was buried therein, and her coffin was found undisturbed in February, 1808, when a child named Mary Chase was laid in a leaden casket beside her. For four years the vault was closed, but in July, 1812, it was opened to admit a Miss Dorcas Chase. The horrified workmen found the coffin of the infant standing on its head in a corner. It was supposed that some mischievous and sacrilegious wretch had been guilty of a senseless outrage, so after the coffin was rearranged the great marble slab was once again placed in position, to be opened next month when a Mr. Chase joined the family group within. During the month there seems to have been no disturbance.

In September, 1816, four years having again elapsed, the vault was opened once more to admit an infant, Samuel Arnes. Once again all was in horrible confusion, and the coffins littered across one another. The affair was now becoming a scandal and the talk of the whole settlement, the whites putting it down to vandalism and the Negroes to ghosts. Once again the vault was closed, and once again, two months later, it was opened to admit Samuel Brewster. Crowds followed the coffin and gathered round the vault when the great slab was pushed aside. In the short interval everything had again been disarranged, the coffins being abominably mishandled. Mrs. Goddard's coffin, which seems to have been of wood, was broken, but this may have been natural decay. The leaden coffins were scattered at all angles. Once again they were reverently collected, the wooden coffin was tied up, and the vault secured.

Three years later, on July 7th, 1819, Miss Clarke was to be buried in the vault. So great was the public excitement that the governor, Lord Combermere, of Peninsula fame, attended the ceremony with his staff and aides-de-camp. Things were as bad as ever. The wooden coffin was intact, but the others were scattered in all directions. Lord Combermere was so interested that he had the whole structure searched and sounded, but there was no hidden approach or underground passage. It was an insoluble mystery. The coffins were rearranged and the floor carefully sanded so that footsteps would be revealed. The door was cemented up, which seems to have been done on each occasion, but this time the Governor affixed his own particular seal. The British Government had officially entered the lists against the powers of darkness.

It is humiliating to add that the powers of darkness seemed not in the least abashed either by the Governor or by the Empire which he represented. Next year, in April 1820, it was determined that an official inspection should be made without waiting for a fresh interment. Lord Combermere with a formidable official party and a strong ally in the Rev. T. Orderson, rector of the parish, repaired to the vault, where the seals were found intact and all in apparent order. The cement was then broken and the slab removed by the exertions of ten Negroes, who had the utmost difficulty in forcing an entrance. On exposing the interior it was found to the horror and amazement of the party that the difficulty in opening the vault had been caused by the fact that a leaden coffin within, so heavy that several men could hardly move it, had been jammed upside down against the slab. There was great confusion within but no marks upon the sand which covered the floor. So horrified was everyone by this final test that the bodies were now removed and buried elsewhere. The empty vault remains, and is likely for many centuries to remain, as a refuge for snakes or centipedes, upon the lonely headland which overlooks the Atlantic.

What is one to make of such a story as that? The facts seem to be beyond question. Are there any points which are particularly to be noted from a psychic point of view, in the hope that the germs of law may lie within? One is that the antipathy of those unseen forces was aroused apparently by the *leaden* coffins. When the wooden coffin was alone it was not molested. Its decay seems to have been natural, and when it was tied up it was not again disturbed. If it ever received any injury it may well have been from the weight of the ponderous leaden coffins which were dashed about around it. That is one possible point. A second and more important one is that all psychic phenomena seem to show that the disembodied have no power of their own, but that it is always derived from the emanations of the living, which we call animal magnetism or other names. Now this vault with its absolutely air-tight walls was particularly adapted for holding in such forces— being an exaggerated form of that cabinet which is used for that very purpose by a genuine medium. If the walls of cloth of a cabinet can contain these emanations and condense them, how much more the solid walls of this vault. To bring in these weighty leaden coffins the space must have been crowded with over-heated Negroes, and when the slab was at once hermetically sealed, these effluvia were enclosed and remained behind, furnishing a possible source of that material power which is needful for material effects. These are two points worth noting before we pass on to see if any other such cases may fall into line with this one.

We have not far to seek, for one is quoted in the very book under discussion, with a reference to the *European Magazine* for September, 1815, under the heading "The Curious vault at Stanton in Suffolk." In the magazine account it says:

On opening the vault some years since, several leaden coffins with wooden cases that had been fixed on biers, were found displaced to the great astonishment of many. The coffins were placed as before, when some time ago, another of the family dying, they were a second time found displaced. Two years after they were found not only all off the biers, but one coffin as heavy as to require eight men to raise it was found on the fourth step that leads into the vault.

There unhappily the information ends. It tallies very closely with the West Indian case so far as it goes, but is far weaker as regards the evidence and the details. I have made inquiry from the present vicar of the parish but have been unable to improve either the one or the other. The statement that the phenomenon occurred twice and the precise information as to this situation of the coffin upon the fourth step of the stairs, seem to remove the story from vague rumour and show that it was based upon some actual fact.

The next case, however, is fuller and more circumstantial. It comes from the Livonian village of Ahrensburg in the Baltic, and remote as the scene is, the evidence is well attested.

There is a considerable cemetery in the village, which is dotted with small private chapels, each of them with a family burial vault beneath it. The finest of these belonged to a family named Buxhoewden which faced the public high road, and contained certain posts to which the horses of the farmers used to be haltered when the owners were occupied in the town. The first signs of anything peculiar lay in the behaviour of these creatures, which showed such symptoms of terror that they attracted the notice of passers-by. They were covered with sweat, trembled all over, and in three cases actually died from the violence of their emotion. At the same time certain loud but vague sounds were heard to come either from the chapel or from the vault beneath it. These portents were in the early summer of the year 1844.

In July a member of the Buxhoewden family died, and the hearse horses on approaching the cemetery showed the same signs of terror as the others. The service in the chapel was interrupted by hollow groans, which may have been imagined by a congregation who were already predisposed to alarm. What was not imagination, however, was the fact that those who afterwards descended into the vault found the coffins there, which had been in rows, cast into a confused heap upon the wooden floor. These coffins seem to have been of massive oak, very strongly and heavily made. This might have been the work of some enemy to the family, but the doors of the vault had been secured and the locks were intact. There was always the possibility of false keys, however, so the coffins were replaced in their order, and the place very carefully secured.

As the agitation of the horses and the general unrest of the community still continued the chief man of the district, Baron de Guldenstubbe, took up the matter officially, and so the Russian Government found itself involved in the same onesided contention from which the Governor of Barbados had gained so little satisfaction. With two of his family he made a preliminary examination, and then finding the coffins once again in confusion, he formed a committee of investigation consisting of himself, the local bishop, the Bürgermeister, a physician named Luce and four representative citizens.

On entering the vault they again found that the enemy had been at work and that the contents were scattered in all directions. Only three coffins, those of a very saintly grandmother and of two little children, were undisturbed. Attempted robbery was suggested as an explanation, which was the more plausible as an adjoining vault had once been entered, and some gold fringe taken from the coffins. But nothing was now missing nor was there any means of entrance. The committee pursued its research with great care, even to the point of opening some coffins to see if rings and trinkets buried with the owners were still within. It was found that this was so. Workmen were then called in to examine the floor and walls, but no secret entrance could be discovered.

Everything was now closed up once more and the disconsolate committee withdrew, after placing heavy seals upon the door. Before leaving the vault fine ashes were scattered all over the wooden floor, and also over the steps leading down, and the pavement of the chapel. Finally guards were set for three days and nights. It must be admitted that they did things thoroughly in the village of Ahrensburg. At the end of that time the Commission returned in full state with the whole population lining the churchyard rails, eager to hear the result.

The seals were unbroken, the door unopened, but the interior of the vault was in the usual state of chaos. No sign at any point was found upon the ashes and no human feet had entered, but great forces had none the less been at work. The secret powers, reinforced rather than abashed by the recent visit of the Commission, had wrought far greater mischief than before. All the coffins were scattered, save the same three which had been exempt before. Some of the heaviest had been placed upside-down so that the corpse was on its head, and in one instance the lid had burst and the right arm of the inmate, who was a man who had died by his own hand, was protruding and pointing towards the ceiling. Such was the fearsome spectacle which greeted the Commission. They were duly noted in a detailed report and are still to be consulted among the official records of the Island of Oesel, with the names of the witnesses attached. It is also on record that the effect upon the mind of Dr. Luce, who was a man of considerable attainments and a Voltairian in religion, was a complete change of mental outlook, and that revulsion from materialism which any actual contact with the spiritual world, even in its crudest forms, must logically produce.

The result of these gruesome phenomena was that the coffins were removed from the vault and were buried in earth, after which complete tranquillity seems to have descended upon the little village. Not only were there no disturbances to vex the population, but the horses were observed to occupy their old stance without any symptoms of terror. Nothing was left of the whole incident save a memory, but it was a memory which should not be allowed to die, for the facts are really as well attested as facts could be. Apart from the official record, Mr. Dale Owen, who was American minister to Naples and a man of great intelligence, met Miss de Guldenstubbe and her brother in 1859 and took their personal recollections of the whole matter. It is from his work that I have taken the details.

No doubt many other such cases could be recorded, but here at least are three which appear to be authentic and which reproduce the same characteristics. If relics of some strange animal were found in three different localities, the first conclusion among men of science would be that such an animal did exist, and was henceforth to be included among the creatures of earth. The next proceeding would be to compare the relics and to endeavour to reconstruct some image of the new-comer. In the same way these three cases may be said to fairly establish the fact of these curious phenomena which involve the desecration of graves—a fact which, however gruesome, does at least strike at the very roots of that material view of life which has been so fashionable. When we come to compare the cases, however, and to deduce the underlying laws, the psychic student can at best only point to a few possible indications which may be of value.

It has already been stated that one or more living people in a confined space which is afterwards closed up may leave behind them something human and yet invisible, which is sufficiently subtle to be used by forces from the other side as a basis for material phenomena. All movements of solid objects, touched or untouched, in the presence of a medium are to be explained in this fashion, and the force may be expected to be stronger when confined within a limited space. In the case of the Cheriton dug-out, which occupied public attention a couple of years ago, the worker and the boy were busy in a narrow excavation. One or other was mediumistic—that is to say, emitted to an unusual extent this emanation—with the result that the phenomena occurred in the same way, though with less force, when both of them had left the work for their luncheon, as Mr. Jaques, the owner of the property, was able to testify. Let us suppose that in the case of each of these three vaults there was an accumulation of this mysterious, but very certain, power left behind by the coffin-bearers, and possibly reinforced by the committees of inquiry, who would have been very amazed had they been told that they were, in all probability, themselves contributing to the phenomena. There, I think, you have the physical basis which is necessary for every spiritual manifestation, for it cannot too often or too clearly be insisted upon that spirits are not omnipotent and irresponsible forces, but that they are under a rule of law no less strict than our own. One of these laws is that a physical basis is needed for every physical manifestation. We may find in the future some non-human basis, for it is conceivable that some subtle chemical action could be established which would generate this magnetic force just as zinc and acid generate the kindred mystery of electricity. But a physical basis there must be. No ghost was ever self-supporting. He can exist without our help, but he cannot manifest to human eyes without drawing his material from human (or possibly animal) sources. That, as it seems to me, is one of the basic laws of the new world of science.

There is some evidence, which could be cited in full if it did not lead us down a lengthy side street, that when a life has been cut short before it has reached its God-appointed term, whether the cause be murder or suicide (of accident I speak with less confidence), there remains a store of unused vitality which may, where the circumstances are favourable, work itself off in capricious and irregular ways. This is, I admit, a provisional theory, but it has been forced upon my mind by many considerations. Such a theory would go some way to explain, or at least to throw some dim light upon, the disturbances which from all past time have been associated with scenes of violence and murder. If it could be conceived that the unseen part of a man is divisible into the higher, which passes on as spirit, and the lower which represents animal functions and mere unused vitality, then it is this latter which has not been normally worked off in a life prematurely ended, and which may express itself in strange semi-intelligent fashion afterwards. In dreams one is conscious of some such division, where the higher functions occasionally bring us back touches of the most spiritual; while the lower functions, deprived for the time of judgment, humour and all the spirit qualities, evolve a capricious and grotesque life of their own, which has neither reason nor sense of proportion and yet seems very real to us in our slumbers. It is not a subject upon which one could be dogmatic,

88

but the days are passing when all such cases can be disposed of by being brushed aside and ignored as senseless superstition. Some sort of framework must be formed into which they can be fitted, and with fuller knowledge the fit will be closer.

Finally the question arises: What was the object of such phenomena? We see that the result in at least two cases out of three was that the dead were buried elsewhere. Apparently for some reason the earth burial may have been desired instead of the seclusion of the vault. It would certainly hasten the absolute decomposition of the body, if that should be good from the point of view of the other world. This seems a far-fetched supposition and one very much at variance with the belief of those numerous nations who have practised the art of embalming and corpse-preservation, but if this was not the object of the disturbance it must be admitted that it is difficult to see what other result was attained, save a very compelling proof of unseen intelligences and powers. If a speedy decomposition was the object aimed at, then the leaden and heavy oak coffins would check the process, which would be swifter in the more fragile wooden ones. This might conceivably explain the particular violence which seems to have been used towards the more permanent materials. Perhaps, however, we lose time in searching for rational explanations, since there is ample evidence that there can be rowdiness and hooliganism beyond the veil as well as here.

One remark should be made before passing on to another form of ghostly manifestation. It has been said that the basis for physical results lies in the human organism. It is not meant, however, that there is any relation between the small amount often taken from the medium and the great physical results obtained. It is clear that the unseen forces can get great power from a limited supply of this subtle material. In the case carefully observed and noted by Professor Zöllner of Leipzig, a beam of wood which two horses could not have dragged apart was shattered into pieces in the presence of Slade. A friend of mine who was present at a meeting of the Goligher circle saw a table ascend in the air and remain there, although four strong men did all they could to drag it down. It is true that in a sitting of this sort the medium, Miss Goligher, frequently registered a loss of weight amounting to a stone in a séance upon the weighing-dial which Dr. Crawford had erected, but it is clear that the force exerted by the unseen powers was very much greater than this and was due to their own manipulation of the material which her organism had provided. In some of the sittings of D. D. Home, the force was so great that the whole building used to shake as if a heavy train were passing below it.

And here comes one of the mysteries which bear directly upon that definition of spirit law which is so desirable. In spite of the possibility of using vast power there is a clear, and so far as credible records go, an unbroken ordinance that a ghost may not for its own personal ends destroy anything or injure anyone. This may seem in contradiction to the broken coffins, but that may not have been for personal ends, but an accident due to the falling about of the heavy weights. Here is an authentic case in illustration:

A great friend of mine, a Roman Catholic priest, whose word could not be doubted by anyone who knew him, was sent for a rest cure to a lonely house upon the coast which was frequently used by other priests for the same purpose. Save for an old crone and one or two charitable visitors, he was absolutely alone. After a few days he became conscious of strange noises in the house, which at last reached such a point that, to quote his own description, "it sounded at night as if there were a steam-engine snorting and clanking in the room below." Nothing was visible, but the sounds were incessant and were heard by two visitors as clearly as by the inmate. The priest is himself open more than most men to psychic impressions, and upon that night he had a dream or vision which was so absolutely clear that he determined to act upon it. He descended in the morning and asked the old woman whether there was not an unused room in the basement. She answered that there was. He entered it and found that he had already seen it in his dream—a small dusty, cobwebbed place with some old books of theology heaped in the corners. He walked at once to one of these heaps, picked up a book as in his dream, opened it, took out a sheet of written paper, glanced at it to make sure that it was really as revealed and then carried it into the kitchen, where he stuffed it between the bars of the grate. The paper was a written preparation for confession, made out by some over-conscientious or over-methodical inmate of the house, who had noted down a good many more things than were desirable for public perusal. Presumably he had died shortly afterwards and had been worried by the recollection of this document, which he then took these means to have destroyed. There were no further disturbances of any sort within the house.

Now here is a story which is undoubtedly true and which cannot be met by any of the ingenious explanations of the honest but sceptical

Researcher. If the subconscious knowledge of my friend could have told him that the paper was there, it certainly could not have caused the noises which alarmed him. It has to be examined as a fact, as the zoologist already quoted would examine the skin of his rare animal. The unhappy spirit could apparently draw power either from the old housekeeper or, as is more likely, from the young and psychic priest, to shake the very house with vibrations, and yet with all this power he could not destroy a frail sheet of paper, but had to bring its destruction about in this indirect fashion. This seems to be a solid and noteworthy conclusion. All authentic tales where spirits linger, earth-bound because they appear to be worried over earthly things, concealed treasure, lost documents, or other such matters, come into this category, and the question which one naturally asks, "Why can't they set the matter right for themselves?" is answered by, "They have not the power. It is against the law."

I believe that all these varied experiences have been sent to us not to amuse us by tales to be told and then forgotten but as the essential warp and woof of a new spiritual garment which is to be woven for the modern world. We live in an age which has long demanded a sign, yet when the sign was sent it was blind to it. I cannot understand the frame of mind of those who view proofs of survival which appear in the Bible as of most vital importance, and yet close their mind to the same thing when they reappear before our very eyes. I believe most of the evidence in the sacred books, where it is not perverted by mistranslation, interposition or forgery, to be perfectly good evidence, but no honest mind could say that judged by human standards of credibility it could, for an instant, compare in its demonstration of the fate which awaits the soul, with the psychic revelations of recent years. In the latter case the witnesses are thousands in number, are men of the highest credibility, and have placed in many cases their personal experiences upon record so that any objection can be lodged. Modern Britain does not disprove but confirms ancient Judea. We are in a more scientific age, however, and we wish to know the how and the why. Such inquiries are no longer, with so great a wealth of material, beyond the scope of our brains. In this article I have endeavoured to indicate two well-marked laws: the one that it is the effluvia of the human organism which furnish the basis of physical manifestations from the unseen;

the other, that there is a strict limitation of psychic power which does not prevent noise and subsequent disturbance, but does stand in the way of destruction or personal violence.

This power of producing noise and commotion may, it is true, cause such great misery to those who endure it that it may amount to mental torture. There is the well-known case of Miss Clavion, the famous French actress, who refused the advances of a young Breton suitor. The man died two years later with menaces against Miss Clavion upon his lips. He was as good as his word and proved the wisdom of her rejection by the unmanly persecution to which he subjected her after his death. This took the form of loud cries, which frequently broke out when she was in the company of others, and were so terrible that some of the hearers fainted. In the later stages of her persecution these cries gave place to the sound of a musket going off, which occurred once a day through a particular window of her house. On ninety days running this phenomenon occurred, and was most fully investigated as the cries had also been, by the Parisian police, who placed spies in the street and sought constantly but in vain for any normal explanation. Finally, after two years the persecution stopped, the time having been foretold by the dead man, who declared that he would upset her life for the same period as she had upset his. He had certainly done so, but like all revenge, it was probably a two-edged knife which cut him more deeply than his victim.

A more justifiable persecution, but one which also amounted to torture, is detailed by Mrs. Carter Hall, the authoress, as having come within her personal observation in her youth. In this case a young officer had inflicted the greatest of all injuries upon a beautiful young woman, who afterwards died. The resulting persecution may have come not from her gentle spirit, but from that of someone who loved her and desired to avenge her, but it was of the most atrocious character. Particulars will be found in Mr. Dale Owen's *Footfalls*—a book so accurate in its cases and so wise in its deductions that it should be a classic upon this subject. The unfortunate officer was attended wherever he went by such noises and disturbances that at last no landlady would let rooms to him, and he was hunted from house to house, a miserable and despairing man, alternately praying for relief and cursing at his unseen enemy. No dog would stay with him, and even his relatives were scared at his company, so that he had to leave his home for fear of driving his mother and sister into an asylum. "It is hard to be so punished," he said to Mrs. Carter Hall, "but perhaps I have deserved it." Possibly this admission may have proved to be the dawn of better days.

VI

THE ALLEGED POSTHUMOUS
WRITINGS OF
KNOWN AUTHORS

OSCAR WILDE—JACK LONDON—
LORD NORTHCLIFFE—DICKENS
—CONRAD—JEROME

FROM TIME TO TIME communications have come through mediums which are alleged to emanate from men who have been famous in literature. These have been set aside by the ordinary critic, who starts with the assumption that the thing is in a general sense absurd, and therefore applies the same judgment with little or no examination to the particular case. Those of us, however, who have found that many psychic claims have actually been made good, may be inclined to look a little more closely into these compositions, and judge how far, from internal evidence, the alleged authorship is possible or absurd. I venture to say that an impartial critic who approached the subject from this angle will be rather surprised at the result.

Let us predicate on the first instance that if the Spiritualist hypothesis is true, and if things are carried out exactly as they say, then one would expect the posthumous work to be inferior to that of the living man. In the first place, he is filtering it through another brain which may often misinterpret or misunderstand. Even a typewriter under my own control, causes me, I find, to lose something of my sureness of touch, and how much more would it be if it were an unstable human machine which I was endeavouring to operate. In the second place, the writer has entered upon a new life with a new set of experiences, and with the tremendous episode of physical dissolution between him and the thoughts of earth. This also may well show itself in his style and diction. The most that we can hope for is something which is strongly reminiscent of the deceased writer. This, of course, might be produced by parody, and we have to ask ourselves how far such a parody is likely or even possible in the case of the particular medium. If that medium has never shown signs of the rare power of parody, if he has had no previous literary experience, and if there are other internal evidences of the author's identity, then the case becomes a stronger one. In no event could judgment be absolutely final, but if several instances can be adduced, each of which is cogent, then the collective effect would tend to greatly strengthen the psychic proof of identity.

I would first take the alleged messages of Oscar Wilde, which are certainly very arresting. Wilde's style was so marked, and at its best so remarkably beautiful, that I have never seen any admitted parody which was adequate. Yet there have been several communications alleged to be from the other side which do reproduce those peculiarities in a very marked form. One of these was a play which came through the hand of Mrs. Hester Dowden, and which exhibited both the strength and the weakness of Wilde. Another is to be found in that remarkable narrative, "Both Sides of the Door," where Wilde was alleged to have interfered, in order to save a family who were suffering from a peculiar psychic persecution. Wilde had a particularly fine eye for colour, and a very happy knack of hitting off a tint by an allusion to some natural object. I think that all the "honey-coloured" moons which have floated over recent literature had their origin in one of Wilde's adjectives. In this particular little book Wilde spoke of the Arctic seas as "an ocean of foaming jade." That struck me as a particularly characteristic phrase.

In the present essay, however, we will concentrate our attention upon the volume which has been published by Werner Laurie under the title of *Psychic Messages from Oscar Wilde*. These also came through the hand of Mrs. Dowden (or Mrs. Travers Smith) and they are dignified by a preface from the father of Psychic Research, Sir William Barrett, who makes the general assertion concerning the script, "It does afford strong prima facie evidence of survival after the dissolution of body and brain."

The messages, it should be explained, came partly by automatic writing, while in a normal state, and partly by the ouija board. Mrs. Dowden was associated with Mr. Soal in the experiments, she sometimes working alone, and sometimes with his hands upon the ouija board. Here are some of the messages which seem to me to be most characteristic of Wilde's personality and literary style.

"In eternal twilight I move, but I know that in the world there is day and night, seedtime and harvest, and red sunset must follow apple-green dawn. Every year spring throws her green veil over the world and anon the red autumn glory comes to mock the yellow moon. Already the may is creeping like a white mist over land and hedgerow, and year after year the hawthorn bears blood-red fruit after the death of its may."

This is not merely adequate Wilde. It is exquisite Wilde. It is so beautiful that it might be chosen for special inclusion in any anthology of his writings. The adjective "apple-green" for dawn, and the picture of the may, "creeping like a white mist" are two high lights in a brilliant passage. Again as in the "foaming jade" we have the quick response to colour. It is not too much to say that the posthumous Wilde in such passages as this is Wilde with an added sparkle.

In the script we find that after this passage Wilde was subjected to a long *questionnaire*, which he answered with great precision. When asked why he came, he answered:

"To let the world know that Oscar Wilde is not dead. His thoughts live on in the hearts of all those who in a gross age can hear the flute voice of beauty calling on the hills, or mark where her white feet brush the dew from the cowslips in the morning. Now the mere memory of the beauty of the world is an exquisite pain. I was always one of those for whom the visible world existed. I worshipped at the shrine of things seen. There was not a blood stripe on a tulip or a curve on a shell, or a tone on the sea, but had for me its meaning and its mystery, and its appeal to the imagination.

Others might sip the pale lees of the cup of thought, but for me the red wine of life."

This also is beautiful and rare literary work. If an artist can tell a Rubens by its colouring or a sculptor can assign an ancient statue to Phidias, then I claim that a man with an adequate sense of the rhythm of good prose can ascribe these fine extracts to Wilde and to no one else. His hallmark is stamped upon them for all the world to see, and when it ceases to turn away its head it will see it clearly enough. Immersed in trivialities, it seems to have no leisure at present for the great questions of life and of death.

These two beautiful passages and several others almost as fine, came in a single sitting on June 8th, 1923, and were produced by Mr. Soal writing, while Mrs. Dowden laid her hand upon his. In many forms of mediumship it is to be observed that the blending of two human atmospheres produces finer results than either alone can get.

The cynical humour of Wilde, and a certain mental arrogance which was characteristic, breaks out in these passages.

"Being dead is the most boring experience in life. That is if one excepts being married, or dining with a schoolmaster."

Again being dissatisfied with one of his own images he writes, "Stop! Stop! This image is insufferable. You write like a successful grocer who, from selling pork, has taken to writing poetry."

When someone alluded to an occasion when Whistler had scored off him, he wrote, "With James vulgarity always begins at home."

Again.

"I do not wish to burden you with details of my life, which was like a candle that had guttered at the end. I rather wish to make you believe that I was the medium through which beauty filtered, and was distilled like the essence of a rose."

His literary criticism was acid and unjust, but witty.

"I knew Yeats well—a fantastical mind, but so full of inflated joy in himself that his little cruse of poetry was erupted only with infinite pains over the span of many years."

98

Now and again there are passages of intense interest to an instructed Spiritualist which give a glimpse of the exact sphere upon which Wilde is moving, and the reasons which retard his progress and subject him to those limitations which draw from him the constant exclamation of "Pity Oscar Wilde!" His pictures of earth are a reminiscence, and his witty cynical chatter is a mere screen. The real bitterness of his experience, a bitterness which might I think have been assuaged by some sympathy and instruction from this side, flashes out in occasional passages which vibrate with his emotion.

"I am a wanderer. Over the whole world I have wandered, looking for eyes by which I may see. At times it is given to me to pierce this strange veil of darkness, and through eyes from which my secret must be for ever hidden, gaze once more on the gracious day."

This would mean in our language that from time to time he has been able to take control of a medium, and so get into touch with physical things once more. His troubles come from the desire to struggle down rather than up. He has found strangely assorted mediums.

"I have found sight in the most curious places. Through the eyes out of the dusky face of a Tamil girl I have looked on the tea fields of Ceylon, and through the eyes of a wandering Kurd I have seen Ararat. . . . Once on a pleasure steamer on its way to St. Cloud I saw the green waters of the Seine and the lights of Paris through the vision of a little girl, who clung wondering to her mother and wondered why."

What rational explanation can be given for such messages save the Spiritualistic one? They are there. Whence come they? Are they the unconscious cerebration of Mr. Soal? But many of them have come when that gentleman was not present, so this explanation is ruled out. Are they then an emanation of Mrs. Dowden? But they have come in full strength and beauty when her hands have not been on the ouija board, but have simply touched those of Mr. Soal. What then is the alternative explanation? I confess that I can see none. Can anyone contend that both Mr. Soal and Mrs. Dowden have a hidden strand in their own personality which enables them on occasion to write like a great deceased writer, and at the same time a want of conscience which permits that subconscious strand of actuality to claim that it *is* the deceased author? Such an explanation would seem infinitely more unlikely than any transcendental one can do.

The case might be made fairly convincing on the question of style alone. But there is much more in it than that. The actual writing, which was done at a speed which forbids conscious imitation, is often the handwriting of Wilde, and reproduces certain curious little tricks of spacing which were usual with him in life. He alludes freely to all sorts of episodes, many of them little known, which have been shown to be actual facts. He gives criticisms of authors with a sure, but rather unkind touch, where the medium has little or no acquaintance with the writings criticized. He alludes to people whom he has known in life with the utmost facility. In the case of one, Mrs. Chan Toon, the name was so unlikely that it seemed to me that there must be some mistake. As if to resolve my doubts a letter reached me presently from the very lady herself.

To sum up, I do not think that any person who approached this problem with an open mind can doubt that the case for Wilde's survival and communication is an overpoweringly strong one.

We now turn to a second case, that of Jack London. Here again we are dealing with an author who had such a marked individuality, and such a strong explosive method of expression that any imitation should be readily detected. The collector of the evidence is Edward Payne, who died soon after his task was completed. He was a man of considerable attainments, a close friend of London's in his lifetime, and not a Spiritualist, so we have the material for a very instructed and unprejudiced opinion. The messages came to him through a lady who has a public career, and therefore desires to remain anonymous. Mr. Payne answers for her bona fides, and assures us she was not a professional medium, that she was a woman of considerable culture, and that she was a convinced materialist, so that no strand of her own nature, so far as can be traced, is concerned in producing messages which are in their very nature the strongest indictment of materialism that could be framed.

The messages assume two forms, the one quite unconvincing, the other most powerful. The former is an attempt at a work of fiction which was an utter failure. The fact that London could not get his story of worldly life across, and yet was most convincing in discussing his own actual condition, is to be understood readily. It is clear that he was attempting the most difficult of all forms of communication, a long, connected narrative with characters and plot, under indirect conditions to which no living author could submit. If London had relied upon his transmitted fiction alone he would have been deservedly set down as an impostor. But when he comes to draw not others, but himself, he is much more convincing. Apparently he was much worried after death by finding everything entirely different from anything he had expected, though if he and other materialists would deign to listen to the poor despised Spiritualists they would save themselves all such shocks, the effects of which endure often for many years.

Instead of loss of personality he found himself, like Wilde, in a mist or haze—a reflection of his own perplexed mind—with a body and mind as before, the perceptions being more acute than on earth. He quickly was forced to realize that all his teaching had been utterly wrong, that he had done harm by it, and that his immediate task was to get back if he could, and set the matter right. This getting back is no easy task. The right vibration has to be found, and it is far to seek. But London was not a man to be repulsed. He found his vibration and he delivered his message.

Here are some of the communications which seem to me to bear the stamp of the man on every one of them.

"I am going to try. Trying is the life of me. Ask Aunt Netta if it is Jack who speaks that."

"Here I am alive, feeling myself to be myself, yet nothing I say or write can identify me to those who know me best."

"Death has taught me what earth held from me. My spirit is plunging forward with more vigour than wisdom, as in my earth days. But I know now the way and the life. Oh, I have much, much, that I must undo."

He sends a long, connected communication which is an essay in itself, headed "What Life means to me now." In it he says, "I am a soul —a living Soul. I followed the lost trail of materialism, and sickened in the foul mists of error." The whole composition, which is too long for quotation, is most powerful, and might serve as a warning from the grave, to those millions who so heedlessly tread the very path which led London to his misery.

"My soul, though I knew it not, was dyspeptic with the materialistic fodder I crammed into it. . . . Death caught me unawares. He snapped me up when my face was not turned his way. I almost regret this. I believe it made my transition the harder.

"I awoke. Dreaming? I was sure of it. I dreamed on and on. I dreamed myself into eternity. I am vague. I was vague to myself. My powers returned. I could think. I hailed my old brain like a returned friend. I fumbled and groped. My earth blindness was on me. It hazed me about. I fought my way through it. I had no goal. I had passed the only goal I had ever admitted. I was on the other side of it. I struggle to seize the correct term. I try vainly to translate the experience into terms of earth which has no utterance for it.

"I died. I am looking at death from the other side—the tame friendly side of him. And Life is indestructible. . . . I see man face his destiny as I saw him on earth. I see him fall. I see him rise again and go on. He fights his way and when his place is ready here he comes. There are no catastrophes. All is in order.

"I am a stranger to this tongue. I am but learning to speak. What faculty I possessed on earth is disrupted by a condition it was never trained to meet. I shall strive to re-establish it and then I shall speak, and, friends of earth, you shall recognize my voice."

These short strong pregnant sentences are Jack London at his best. As in the case of Wilde, his posthumous work will bear comparison with anything he has done in life.

He has a horror of his old point of view.

"That which was my truth of yesterday, which I hugged to me as the quintessence of my distilled thought, becomes a volatile poison to me here and I must . . . distil a new thought out of the fires of my previous experience, and by this thought shall I rise. Renaissance of soul is a labour shot with pains of remembrance, held by fetters of past error which are burst with a sweated toil while the heart strains with its propulsion . . . I feel that I have got right with God—I am no longer worshipping myself."

When asked what specific work he was doing, he answered, "I have to direct those lost or bewildered, as I was when I came. I labour to show them the way I would not take."

These last words seem to me to mark the beginning of Jack London's regeneration. He understands that his work is impersonal, unselfish and humble. Before that he had wished to reassert himself on the old earth terms, and the realization that he could not do so was a bitter one. He kicked hard against the pricks.

"God! I am annihilated!" he cried; "my earth life is stamped out, blotted from time by this passage. I can't puzzle it out. My hand fumbles. Did Death rob me as I passed through his clutch. Did he steal the face of me that those who knew me see me strange, feeble, pitiful. Who or what has cut the tap-root of my power? I am befogged."

The child still cried for its toys and refused to understand that it had left the nursery. But it cries in a voice that is familiar. The man himself never spoke in such a vital strain as does his ghost. He ends at last on the note that he is not to look back and that the future only should concern him. "The messages," he said, "come from Jack London, the damned soul, struggling out of his own hell of materialization." But there was light ahead. He had but to persevere. "I am a soldier of the eternal march." Who but Jack London would have written those words? He winds up, "What is more important than to let the world know I am busy undoing what mischief I did." Alas, Jack, the world is too busy with its games and its pleasures, too immersed in its wooden creeds and its petrified religions, to give ear to what you have learned. They, like you, will only realize when it is too late.

It may be gathered from the above that I accept Jack London's return as being a genuine one. I can see no other possible conclusion. The message is there, and it is easier to account for it by the return of London's activities to this sphere, than to torture the theory of multiple personality or subconscious activity, until it is twisted to cover a case which is so much beyond its limits.

There is one other writer who has claimed that he has been able to get messages back to us. This is Lord Northcliffe—or Alfred Harmsworth, as the alleged spirit prefers to be called. In life Harmsworth had no distinctive style, but only the pen of the ready writer, so that it is far more difficult to identify him than in such marked cases as Wilde or London. But if he had not style he had character, and this of a very forcible and individual kind. Judged from that angle his return is convincing, though I would not say it is so conclusive as in the case of the two men of letters.

The great journalist claims to have come through many times, and I have myself had experiences in that direction which cannot possibly be explained away. Hannen Swaffer has given his own account of the matter in his forcible narrative "Northcliffe's Return." For the purpose of this essay, however, I will confine myself to a single long article, said to be dictated by Northcliffe, and coming through the hand of a lady living in a small town in New Zealand, and quite ignorant of her control's character, or of his methods of thought and expression.

He also, like the others, most bitterly regrets the want of true guidance which he had found in his lifetime, and the absorption in material things which stunted his spiritual development. At the same time it is easy to see that the spirit which is struggling for expression is really, as I should judge, upon a higher plane than either of those which have been already discussed. Service is his one ideal and that is the sign of progression. He speaks of his powers humbly enough.

"I would probably not have risen above the rank of private yet had it not been for some executive ability. For the will power and the dynamic force necessary to achieve success in my old line of endeavour has helped me considerably here."

His review of his own earth life is interesting and instructive:

"I had a tremendous lot of power in public affairs, and I now see to how much better use I might have put that power. But I could only act according to my light at the time, and as that light was very dim indeed, on matters pertaining to the more real and lasting things of life, I made many mistakes. We do not suffer for our mistakes, except in witnessing the results of past actions, which is suffering enough in many cases, God knows! What I mean is, that this suffering is self-inflicted, and the only escape from it is in honest toil to try and right some of the wrong we have unwittingly done in the past. In this way only can we wipe the slate clean and start life afresh on a higher level."

Now and again he breaks out into that impetuous and loud-spoken anger which was one of his earth characteristics. Here is an example when he talks of our present misleaders of public opinion:

"The colossal ignorance and arrogant pride of so many of those whose privilege it is to help to form public opinion is my especial bugbear at present. If they would not be so smug and self-satisfied about it I could bear it better. But, as things are, I often long to prick the highly-inflated bubble of their unholy conceit with one of my sharp, old-time, vigorous denunciations of humbug."

And again he has a word to say to those who imagine that to commune with those who are gone can in any way be harmful or disagreeable to those who come to us.

"Poor silly, deluded folks! If they only knew what I, and millions like me know of the heart-hunger for those left behind, which exists over here, they would open their minds and hearts, and make their dear ones as welcome in their lives and concerns as they were before death overtook them. They could do it easily, too, if they would only allow themselves to be properly instructed in these matters of great moment to all concerned, by those who know, instead of being content to listen to those shrill, oft repeated, parrot cries of religious humbugs, who tell of the sin and danger of tampering with these things, whilst knowing nothing whatever of the help and consolation such intercourse can bring to loving, suffering beings on both sides of the veil."

Can anyone imagine that these forceful words, which can be matched in unpublished communications from the same source in England, could have really come from the mind of the lady in far New Zealand.

In the original form of this essay, which appeared in the *Fortnightly Review*, I devoted some space to considering a continuation of *Edwin Drood*, which professed to come from Charles Dickens through the hand of one James who was foreman in a printing office in Brattleborough, Vermont. No one who reads it can deny that it is an excellent imitation of the great author's style, but the most unconvincing part was the narrative itself, which was clumsy and improbable. My conclusion was "that the actual inspiration of Dickens is far from being absolutely established." I added, however, "No one with any critical faculty would say that the result was an entirely unworthy one, though if written by the living Dickens it would certainly not have improved his reputation. It reads," I added, "like Dickens gone flat."

There was an extraordinarily interesting sequel to this. Shortly after I had written as above I had a sitting with Florizel von Reuter the celebrated violin virtuoso, and his mother. Their (or rather her) mediumship is of a most convincing nature, as its technique is in itself of abnormal power. She sits with her eyes tightly bandaged, and her hand upon a small pointer which darts very rapidly at the letters of the alphabet, while her son writes down the result. There is no question at all about the bandage being adequate, and she does not turn her face down to the board. The letters too, are so close together that she could not learn to touch them with accuracy. Yet the messages come through with extreme speed. Whatever their value there is no question that they come in preternatural fashion.

Imagine us there, seated, these two at the centre table, my wife and I in the corner of our cottage room. Dickens and Drood had been in my mind, but our visitors had no means of knowing that. Florizel von Reuter had never read *Edwin Drood*. His mother had read it years ago but had a very vague memory as to the book. Suddenly the pointer begins to dart furiously and Florizel reads off each sentence as he notes it down. Some of them, I may add, came in looking-glass writing and had to be read backwards. The first was, "Boz is buzzing about." Boz, of course, was the nom-de-plume of Dickens, so I asked if it was he. He eagerly declared that it was. After a short interchange of dialogue I said,

"Will you answer some questions?"

"I hope I know enough," was the answer.

"Was that American who finished *Edwin Drood* inspired?"

"Not by me," was the instantaneous and decided answer.

Now von Reuter knew nothing of this matter, and my own opinion was, at the utmost, neutral, so that this positive answer reflected none of our own thoughts.

Then came a further message.

"Wilkie C. did" [or would have done] "better."

There was, I believe, some talk after Dickens' death of Wilkie Collins finishing the book. So far as I know he did nothing in the matter. The von Reuters knew nothing of this.

"Was Edwin Drood dead?"

"No, he was not."

That was certainly my own opinion so I make a present of it to the telepathist.

Then after a pause, the message went on:

"I was sorry to go across before I got him out of his trouble. The poor chap has had a hard time. I don't know which is better, to solve the mystery in your note-book or let it remain a mystery for ever. If you make good with Conrad I will put you on to Edwin."

"I shall be honoured, Mr. Dickens."

"Charles, if you please. We like friends to be friends." The reader will smile at this. So did I. But facts are facts and I am giving them. I asked:

"Have you a clear recollection of the plot?"

"I have."

"Who was Datchery?"

"What about the fourth dimension? I prefer to write it all out through you."

What the fourth dimension has to do with it, I cannot imagine. I think it was meant as chaff, since the fourth dimension is what no one can understand.

Now comes the important sentence:

"Edwin is alive and Chris is hiding him."

This seems to me to be exceedingly important, both from a literary and from a psychic point of view. Some of the best brains in the world have occupied themselves over the problem as to whether Drood was dead, and if not where he could be. Numerous solutions have been suggested, but though I am fairly well posted in the matter this is an entirely new one. Chris is the Rev. Crisparkle, who in the novel is a kindly and energetic, muscular Christian. Certainly if he played the part indicated it is well concealed. But then it was the author's duty to conceal it well. There are several subtle touches which might point to the truth of it. On re-reading the fragment with this idea in my mind I can say with certainty that up to a point Crisparkle certainly knew nothing about it. He has a soliloquy to that effect, and whatever means are legitimate by which an author may mislead a reader, a false soliloquy is not among them. But after that point in the story there is no reason why Crisparkle may not have surprised Drood's secret, and helped him. There was a huge cupboard in Crisparkle's room which is described with a detail which seems unnecessary and exaggerated if nothing is to come from it. There again the artist drew his frontis-piece under Dickens' very particular direction, and it contains small vignettes of various scenes. There is one which shows Drood standing in a sort of vault, and someone who has some indications of clerical garb coming in to him with a lantern. Is this not Crisparkle and is it not some corroboration of the spirit message?

We got no more messages at that time. Let us for a moment, however, consider the case. Is it not clear evidence of an intelligence outside ourselves? I do not insist upon Charles Dickens. If anyone says to me, "How can you prove that it was not an Impersonation?" I would admit frankly that I cannot prove it. There is none of that corroboration from style which I get in the case of Wilde and of London. I put it on the broader basis, "Was it not an Intelligence apart from ourselves?" Whence came an ingenious solution of a mystery which involved a character of which neither of the von Reuters knew anything with a solution entirely new to me. I claim that it was a most evidential case of Intelligence outside our own physical bodies.

I may add that on the same evening we had a number of messages in Arabic which none of us could understand. When, however, I sent them to my friend, Major Marriott, who is a competent Arabic scholar, they proved to be quite correct. This reinforces the argument that the Dickens' messages were quite apart from ourselves.

Before I close my comments upon "dead" authors I might mention two other points of contact which had in each case some evidential value. Both were effected through the von Reuters—once in my presence and once in my absence. In the former case the message, delivered as before by the blindfolded lady, purported to be from Joseph Conrad, whom I had not known in life. He said that he had left a book unfinished, that it dealt with the Napoleonic era, and that he would be glad if I would finish it for him, since he knew that I had worked on that epoch. Neither I nor the von Reuters had any idea that such a book existed. We found on inquiry, however, that it was indeed so, and that the book had actually been published a year or two before in its incomplete form. This, of course, lessens the value of the evidence from a psychic research point of view, since we might have heard of the book and forgotten about it, but the fact remains that none of us had any recollection of it.

On another occasion when I was not present the name "Jerome" came through. On being asked whether it was a Christian or a surname the characteristic answer came:

"It is my alpha and omega."

"I want to speak to Sir Arthur," came next.

"Did you know him in life?"

"Yes, yes, yes" (very excitedly).

"Would you like to write with my son's hand?" He assented eagerly.

Florizel von Reuter, who had the gift of automatic writing, then took the pencil. A message came through that Jerome and I had been good friends, but had disagreed upon the subject of Occultism. The message concluded, "Tell him from me that I know now that he was right and I was wrong. We never know our greatest mistakes at the time we make them. Make it clear to him that I am not dead."

In von Reuter's account of this incident is his remarkable book, *Psychical Experiences of a Musician*, he says:

"I should like to impress upon the reader that neither my mother nor I had the least idea whether Doyle and Jerome had been even superficially acquainted, let alone knowing anything of Jerome's views upon occult matters."

The latter cases are certainly not so convincing as the earlier ones, but if you take all the evidence together it adds, I think, a new and little explored region to psychic research.

VII
SOME CURIOUS PERSONAL EXPERIENCES

MY EXPERIENCES with mediums, good, bad and indifferent, are probably as wide as those of any living man. At one time or another I have experimented with Jonson of Los Angeles, whom I look upon as the best materializing medium whom I have known, with Inez Wagner of the same city, a wonderful voice medium, with Mrs. Wickland and with Miss Besinnet of Toledo, who is also of the first psychic quality. I have sat also in America with Mr. John Ticknor, a gifted amateur; with Mrs. Chenoweth, the famous clairvoyante; with Mrs. Wriedt of Detroit and Valiantine, wonderful direct voice exponents; with "Margery" Crandon, the world-famous amateur; with Miss Ridley of Philadelphia; Mrs. Pruden of Cincinnati; Mrs. Rose Miller of Washington; Mrs. Hazel of Winnipeg; the Hamilton circle in the same city, and many others. In Australasia I experimented with Bailey, the apport medium; Mrs. Susanna Harris; Mrs. Roberts of Dunedin, and several more. In South Africa with Mrs. Kimpton, and half a dozen more. In Paris with "Eva" and with Madame Briffaud. In Denmark with Einar Nielson. In Sweden with the remarkable daughter of Judge Dahl.

At home there are few mediums of the last twenty years whom I have not sampled, including Husk and Craddock of the older generation, and Evan Powell (at his best at the top of the list), Mrs. Roberts, Mrs. Garrett, Mrs. Barkel, Mrs. Brittain (all four splendid clairvoyantes), Mrs. Roberts Johnson and Mrs. Cooper (both of them overworked voice mediums), and a great many others of lesser note.

I have worked also many times with Hope of Crewe, who in his own line is the greatest medium of all time, and with Mrs. Deane, both of them exponents of psychic photography. These are some of the mediums whose gifts I have explored, and in many cases I have sat as often as a dozen times. Hence, if I have formed conclusions they have been based upon wide experiences. I have always taken copious notes of my cases. Fraud I have discovered, and helped to expose in several cases, but on the whole I should not put it at more than ten percent—if as much—of the whole.

With so much practical work behind me the reader can imagine my feelings when in a public debate upon the subject with Dr. Haldane of Cambridge my distinguished opponent said, "I once knew a medium." In my reply I asked him what he would think of me if I contradicted him upon some point of chemistry, and said, "I have once been in a laboratory."

Apart from the ordinary phenomena of the séance room, my life has not given me much direct psychic experience. I have, so far as I know, no spiritual gifts myself and none of that psychic atmosphere which gives a tinge of romance to so many lives. There have, however, been occasions when without the aid of a medium I have been sensitive to the unknown.

One instance occurred some years ago. It was in my bedroom at Crowborough. I wakened in the night with the clear consciousness that there was someone in the room, and that the presence was not of this world. I was lying with my back to the room, acutely awake, but utterly unable to move. It was physically impossible for me to turn my body and face this visitor. I heard measured steps across the room. I was conscious (without seeing it) that someone was bending over me, and then I heard a voice saying in a loud whisper, "Doyle, I come to tell you that I am sorry." A minute later my disability disappeared, and I was able to turn, but all was black darkness and perfectly still. My wife had not awakened, and knew nothing of what had passed.

It was no dream, I was perfectly conscious all the time. My visitor gave no name, but I felt that it was a certain individual to whom I had tried to give psychic consolation when he was bereaved. He rejected my advances with some contempt and died himself shortly afterwards. It may well be that he wished to express regret. As to my own paralysis it came, I have no doubt, from the fact that the power for the manifestation had been drawn out of ME. When spirit manifests upon the physical plane it has to draw its matter from a material source, and I was the obvious one. It is the one occasion upon which I have been used as a physical medium, and I am content that it should be the last.

I had a second interesting experience some years ago. There was a church in the neighbourhood which had the reputation of being haunted. There are reasons why it would be wrong for me to indicate it more precisely. The party consisted of my wife and myself, my two sons, my daughter, a friend, and a young London lady who is among our rising poets. It was ten o'clock when we presented ourselves at the door of the church, where we were met by an elderly villager. Swinging a lantern he led the way to the choir end, where we all seated ourselves in the stalls which the ancient monks once occupied. My own very angular throne was that which had been used by many priors, in far-off days when the old church was one of the shrines of England. Opposite me, and dimly lit by the lantern, was the altar, and behind it a blank wall unbroken by any window, but reflecting strange ghostly shadows and illuminations through the high clerestory windows on either side. When the lantern was extinguished and we sat in the darkness watching these strange shifting lights coming and going, the impression was quite ghostly enough, though I have no doubt at all that there was a physical cause, due to some reflection of passing lights in the distance. It was, however, sufficiently weird.

For two hours I had sat in the dark upon my hard seat, and wondered whether cushions were vouchsafed to the priors of old. The lights still came and went behind the altar, but they only flickered over the top of the high expanse which faced us, and all below was very black. And then suddenly, quite suddenly, there came that which no scepticism could explain away. It may have been forty feet from where I sat to the altar, and midway between, or roughly twenty feet from me, there was a dull haze of light, a sort of phosphorescent cloud, a foot or so across, and about a man's height from the ground. We had been rustling and whispering, but the sudden utter silence showed me that my companions were as tense as I was. The light glimmered down, and hardened into a definite shape—or I should say shapes—since there were two of them. They were two perfectly clear-cut figures in black and white, with a dim luminosity of their own. The colouring and arrangement gave me a general idea of cassocks and surplices. Whether they were facing the altar or facing each other, was more than I could say, but they were not misty figures, but solid objective shapes. For two or three minutes we all gazed at this amazing spectacle. Then my wife said loudly, "Friends, is there anything which we can do to help you?" In an instant they were gone, and we were peering into unbroken darkness with the lights still flickering above.

Personally, I saw no more, but those of our party who sat upon the right, said that they could afterwards see a similar figure, but somewhat taller—a man alone—who stood on the left of the altar. For my own part nothing more occurred, and when midnight tolled forth above our heads, I thought it was time to make for the waiting motor.

Such was our experience. There was no possible room for error. Unquestionably we all saw these figures, and equally unquestionably the figures were not of this world. I was full of curiosity to know more of the matter, and presently my desire was gratified, for there came into my Psychic Bookshop a gentleman, Mr. Munro, who had had a similar experience some years before in the same place. He was possessed, however, of the great gift of clairvoyance, and his adventure was by daylight, so that it was far more definite. He was going round the old church when he was suddenly aware of an ancient monk who was walking by his side, and he knew by his own sensations that it was a clairvoyant vision. The man was middle sized, with a keen, aristocratic, hawk-like face. So clear was he that Mr. Munro remembered how the sunlight shone upon the arched bone of his prominent nose. He walked for some time beside Mr. Munro, and he then vanished. What is noticeable is that he was wearing a gown of a peculiar tint of yellow. Some little time afterwards my informant was present at Bernard Shaw's noble play of "Saint Joan." In one act an English monk appears upon the stage. My friend instantly said to his wife, "That is the dress. That is what the dead man wore." Mrs. Munro, who was in the shop at the time, confirmed this. I may say that they had broached the subject before I had told them of our own experience in the old church.

Then again there came yet another light upon the matter. It was, strange to say, in an Australian paper which was sent to me. It gave an account of the old church, and of the ghosts which haunt it. The chief spirit, the one with the masterful face, was, according to this narrative, the head of the community in the time of Henry the Eighth. He had hid some of the treasures of the church to prevent their spoliation, and his spirit was still earth-bound on account of his solicitude over these buried relics. His name was given, and it was stated that he had shown himself to many visitors. If this account be indeed true, then I should think that the spot in front of the altar, where we saw first the light, and then the two draped figures, might very possibly be worth the attention of the explorer.

I joined the Society for Psychical Research in 1893 or 1894 and must now be one of the oldest members. Shortly afterwards I was asked to form one of a small party to inspect a house at Charmouth. It was said to be haunted.

Dr. Scott of Norwood and Mr. Podmord, a determined and very unreasonable opponent of Spiritualism, were my companions. The evidence in the case was so voluminous that it took us the whole of our railway journey to master it. It consisted mainly of a record of senseless noises which made the place hardly habitable for the unfortunate family who had it on a lease and could not afford to abandon it.

They proved to be charming people. An elderly mother, a grown-up son and a married daughter.

The house was a rambling place, a couple of centuries old. We sat up for two nights. On the first nothing occurred. On the second Dr. Scott left us, and I sat alone with Mr. Podmord and the young man. We had, of course, taken every precaution to checkmate fraud, put worsted thread across the stairs, and so on.

We had just begun to think that the second night would be as blank as the first and the ladies had already gone to bed when a fearsome noise broke out. It was like someone whacking a table with a heavy stick. The door of the sitting-room was open and the noise reverberated down the passage.

We rushed into the kitchen from which the sound appeared to come, but there was nothing to be seen there, and the threads on the stair were unbroken. The others returned to the sitting-room, but I remained waiting in the dark in the hope that the noise would break out once more.

There was, however, no return and we were never able to cast a light upon the mystery. We could only say that what we had heard corroborated, up to a point, what we had read in the account of the disturbances.

There was, however, a curious sequel. Within a year or so the house was burnt down, which may or may not have had a connection with the mischievous sprite who appeared to haunt it. A suggestive thing, however, was that the skeleton of a child about ten years old was dug up in the garden. This I had from relatives of the family who were so plagued.

Some people think that a young life cut short in an unnatural fashion may leave, as it were, a store of unused vitality which may be put to strange uses.

I was never asked by the Society for a report of this case, but Podmord sent one in, ascribing the noises to the young man, though as a matter of fact, he was actually sitting with us in the parlour when the trouble began. Therefore, the explanation given by Podmord was absolutely impossible. I think that if we desire truth we should not only be critical of all psychic assertions, but equally so of all so-called exposures in this subject. I am sorry to say that in some cases the exposure means downright fraud upon the part of the critic.

One other curious experience comes back to my memory. Shortly after the War I had a letter from the widow of a distinguished soldier living at Alton, Hampshire, in which she stated that her life was made miserable by a noisy haunting of her house, which frightened the children and drove away the servants.

I visited her, however, to see what I could do. She had taken it as a furnished house with a lease of some years, and it was impossible for her to leave it.

I found that the lady was, herself, very psychic, and had the power of automatic writing. Through this it was that she received the name of the entity which haunted the house and she assured me that on making inquiries she found, after some time, that a person of that name had actually inhabited the house some sixty years before. On asking him why his spirit should be so restless she received the answer that some papers about which he was anxious were concealed in the rafters of the box-room.

This message had actually just come through and the box-room had not yet been explored. It was a terrible place, thick with dust and piled with all kinds of lumber, and for an hour or more, in my shirt and trousers, I crawled about under the rafters looking for these papers. I observed, however, that at some period, a bell wire had been passed along there, and it was clear to me that the men who fixed the wire would certainly have come upon any concealed packet. I therefore, made my way back to the sitting-room in a shocking state of dust and perspiration and then and there the lady and I held a table-sitting in which I addressed the unseen entity and explained to him that the papers, if they had ever been there, were certainly gone.

I remonstrated with him for the trouble which he had given to the household and I begged him to think no more of his worldly affairs, but to attune his mind to the higher life. When I asked him if he would do so the table spelt D.V.

I am conscious that this is very vague and open to criticism, but the direct sequel of it all was that from that day onwards the trouble entirely ceased, and the lady was able to write and to assure me that the atmosphere of her house had changed to one of deep peace.

Thus my visit to Alton was not entirely in vain.

VIII

DWELLERS ON THE BORDER[1]

I PROPOSE in this essay to discuss the evidence for the existence of elemental forms of life, invisible to the normal eye, which inhabit the same planet as ourselves. It seems to me that our knowledge of the ether vibrations which govern wireless are a great help to us in this connection, and that we can readily understand now what would have been incomprehensible, because there was no existing analogy, a few years ago. Let us suppose that the London centre was the only one known, and that we were in touch with it through our own receiving apparatus. That represents our reaction to the material world and normally we know of no other, just as the wireless recipient would know only London. But we find that by a very small change of vibration or wave-length we get Paris, Berlin, or Constantinople, and London has vanished. Now if we apply that to psychic vibrations the analogy seems to me very close. As Paracelsus said, "Ut infra, ita supra" (As it is below so it is above). A uniformity runs through the scheme of creation. The clairvoyant whose various powers of receptivity enable him to contact different types of extra-corporeal creatures, corresponds to the man who can switch from one centre to another, and he has the same difficulty in getting his results accepted as the owner of a wave-adjustment set would have if all the normal world was confined to one vibration.

[1] An expansion of this general argument is to be found in *The Coming of the Fairies* (Psychic Press, 2 Victoria Street, W.).

To vary the simile, we are accustomed to the idea of amphibious creatures who may dwell unseen and unknown in the depths of the waters, and then some day be spied sunning themselves upon a sandbank, whence they slip into the unseen once more. If such appearances were rare, and if it should so happen that some saw them more clearly than others, then a very pretty controversy would arise, for the sceptics would say with every show of reason, "Our experience is that only land creatures live on the land, and we utterly refuse to believe in things which slip in and out of the water; if you will demonstrate them to us we will begin to consider the question." Faced by so reasonable an opposition the others could only mutter that they had seen them with their eyes, but that they could not command their movements. The sceptics would hold the field.

Something of the sort may exist in our psychic arrangements. One can well imagine that there is a dividing line, like the water edge, this line depending upon what we vaguely call a higher rate of vibrations. Taking the vibration theory as a working hypothesis, one could conceive that by raising or lowering them, creatures could move from one side to the other of this line of material visibility, as the tortoise moves from the water to the land, returning for refuge to invisibility as the reptile scuttles back to the surf. This, of course, is supposition, but intelligent supposition based on the available evidence is the pioneer of science, and it may be that the actual solution will be found in this direction. I am alluding, now, not to spirit return, where eighty years of close observation have given us some sort of certain and definite laws, but rather of those fairy and phantom phenomena which have been endorsed by so many ages, and even in these material days seem to break into some lives in the most unexpected fashion. Victorian science would have left the world hard and clean and bare, like a landscape in the moon, but this science is in truth but a little light in the darkness, and outside that limited circle of definite knowledge we see the loom and shadow of gigantic and fantastic possibilities around us, throwing themselves continually across our consciousness in such ways that it is difficult to ignore them.

There is much curious evidence of varying value concerning these borderland forms, which come or go either in fact or imagination—the latter most frequently no doubt. And yet there remains a residue which by all human standards should point to occasional facts. I pass in this essay the age-long tradition which is so universal and consistent, and come down to some modern instances which make one feel that this world is very much more complex than we had imagined, and that there may be upon its surface some very strange neighbours who will open up inconceivable lines of science for our posterity, especially if it should be made easier for them, by sympathy or other help, to emerge from the deep and manifest upon the margin.

Taking a large number of cases of fairy lore which lie before me, there are two points which are common to nearly all of them. One is that children claim to see these creatures far more frequently than adults. This may possibly come from greater sensitiveness of apprehension, or it may depend upon these little entities having less fear of molestation from the children. The other is that more cases are recorded in which they have been seen in the still shimmering hours of a very hot day than at any other time. "The action of the sun upon the brain," the sceptic says. Possibly—and also possibly not. If it were a question of raising the slower vibrations of our surroundings one could imagine that still heat would be the condition which might favour such a change. What is the mirage of the desert? What is that scene of hills and lakes which a whole caravan can see while it faces in a direction where for a thousand miles of desert there is neither hill nor lake, nor any cloud or moisture to produce refraction? I can ask the question but I do not venture to give an answer. It is clearly a phenomenon which is not to be confused with the erect or often inverted image which is seen in a land of clouds and of moisture.

There are many people who have a recollection of these experiences of their youth and try afterwards to explain them away on material grounds which do not seem adequate or reasonable. Thus in his excellent book on Folklore the Rev. S. Baring-Gould gives us a personal experience which illustrates several of the points already mentioned.

"In the year 1838," he says, "when I was a small boy, four years old, we were driving to Montpelier on a hot summer day over the long straight road that traverses a pebble and rubble-strewn plain on which grows nothing save a few aromatic herbs. I was sitting on the box with my father when to my great surprise I saw legions of dwarfs of about two feet high running along beside the horses—some sat laughing on the pole, some were scrambling up the harness to get on the backs of the horses. I remarked to my father what

I saw, when he abruptly stopped the carriage and put me inside beside my mother, where, the conveyance being closed, I was out of the sun. The effect was that little by little the host of imps diminished in numbers till they disappeared altogether."

Here certainly the advocates of sunstroke have a strong though by no means a final case. Mr. Baring-Gould's next illustration is a stronger one.

"When my wife was a girl of fifteen," he says, "she was walking down a lane in Yorkshire between hedges, when she saw seated in one of the privet hedges a little green man, perfectly well made, who looked at her with his beady, black eyes. He was about a foot or fifteen inches high. She was so frightened that she ran home. She remembers that it was a summer day."

A girl of fifteen is old enough to be a good witness, and her fright and the clear detail of her memory point to a real experience. Again we have the suggestion of a hot day.

Baring-Gould has yet a third case.

"One day a son of mine," he says, "was sent into the garden to pick pea-pods for the cook to shell for dinner. Presently he rushed into the house as white as chalk to say that while he was thus engaged, and standing between the rows of peas, he was a little man wearing a red cap, a green jacket, brown knee-breeches, whose face was old and wan, and who had a grey beard and eyes as black and hard as sloes. He stared so intently at the boy that the latter took to his heels."

Here again the pea-pods show that it was summer and probably in the heat of the day. Once again the detail is very exact and corresponds closely, as I shall presently show, to some independent accounts. Mr. Baring-Gould is inclined to put all these down to the heat conjuring up the familiar pictures of fairy-books, but some further evidence may cause the reader to doubt this explanation.

Let us compare with these stories the very direct evidence of Mrs. Violet Tweedale, whose courage in making public the result of her own remarkable psychic faculties should meet with recognition from every student of the subject. Our descendants will hardly realize the difficulty which now exists of getting first-hand evidence with names attached, for they will have outgrown the state when the cry of "fake" and "fraud" and "dupe" is raised at once against any observer, however honourable and moderate, by people who know little or nothing of the subject. Mrs. Tweedale says:

"I had a wonderful little experience some five years ago which proved to me the existence of fairies. One summer afternoon I was walking alone along the avenue of Lupton House, Devonshire. It was an absolutely still day—not a leaf moving, and all nature seemed to sleep in the hot sunshine. A few yards in front of me my eye was attracted by the violent movements of a single long, blade-like leaf of a wild iris. This leaf was swinging and bending energetically while the rest of the plant was motionless. Expecting to see a field mouse astride it I stepped very softly up to it. What was my delight to see a tiny green man. He was about five inches long and was swinging back downwards. His tiny green feet which appeared to be green-booted were crossed over the leaf and his hands, raised behind his head, also held the blade. I had a vision of a merry little face and something red in the form of a cap on the head. For a full minute he remained in view, swinging on the leaf. Then he vanished. Since then I have several times seen a single leaf moving violently while the rest of the plant remained motionless, but I have never again been able to see the cause of the movement."

Here the dress of the fairy, green jacket and red cap, is exactly the same as was described independently by Baring-Gould's son, and again we have the elements of heat and stillness. It may be fairly answered that many artists have drawn the fairies in such a dress, and that the colours may in this way have been impressed upon the minds of both observers. In the bending iris we have something objective, however, which cannot easily be explained away as a cerebral hallucination, and the whole incident seems to me an impressive piece of evidence.

A lady with whom I have corresponded, who is engaged in organizing work of the most responsible kind, has had an experience which resembles that of Mrs. Tweedale.

"My only sight of a fairy," she says, "was in a large wood in West Sussex about nine years ago. He was a little creature about half a foot high dressed in leaves. The remarkable thing about his face was that no soul looked through his eyes. He was playing about in long grass and flowers in an open space."

Once again summer is indicated. The length and colour of the creature correspond with Mrs. Tweedale's account, while the lack of soul in the eyes may be compared with the "hard" eyes described by young Baring-Gould.

One of the most gifted clairvoyants in England was the late Mr. Turvey of Bournemouth, whose book, *The Beginnings of Seership*, should be in the library of every student. Mr. Lonsdale of Bournemouth is also a well-known sensitive. The latter has given me the following account of an incident which he observed some years ago in the presence of Mr. Turvey.

"I was sitting," says Mr. Lonsdale, "in his company in his garden at Branksome Park. We sat in a hut which had an open front looking on to the lawn. We had been perfectly quiet for some time, neither talking nor moving, as was often our habit. Suddenly I was conscious of a movement on the edge of the lawn, which on that side went up to a grove of pine trees. Looking closely I saw several little figures dressed in brown peering through the bushes. They remained quiet for a few minutes, and then disappeared. In a few seconds a dozen or more small people about two feet in height, in bright clothes and with radiant faces, ran on to the lawn, dancing hither and thither. I glanced at Turvey to see if he saw anything and whispered, 'Do you see them?' He nodded. These fairies played about, gradually approaching the hut. One little fellow, bolder than the others, came to a croquet hoop close to the hut, and using the hoop as a horizontal bar, turned round and round it, much to our amusement. Some of the others watched him, while others danced about, not in any set dance, but seemingly moving in sheer joy. This continued for four or five minutes, when suddenly, evidently in response to some signal or warning from those dressed in brown, who had remained at the edge of the wood, they all ran into the wood. Just then a maid appeared coming from the house with tea. Never was tea so unwelcome, as evidently its appearance was the cause of the disappearance of our little visitors."

Mr. Lonsdale adds, "I have seen fairies several times in the New Forest, but never so clearly as this." Here also the scene is laid in the heat of a summer day, and the division of the fairies into two different sorts is remarkably borne out by the general descriptions.

Knowing Mr. Lonsdale as I do to be a responsible, well-balanced, and honourable man, I find such evidence as this very hard to put to one side. Here, at least, the sunstroke hypothesis is negatived since both men sat in the shade of the hut and each corroborated the observation of the other. On the other hand, each of the men, like Mrs. Tweedale, was supernormal in psychic development, so that it might well happen that the maid, for example, would not have seen the fairies even if she had arrived earlier upon the scene.

I know a gentleman belonging to one of the learned professions whose career would not be helped if this article were to connect him with fairy lore. As a matter of fact, in spite of his solemn avocations and his practical and virile character, he seems to be endowed with that faculty—let us call it the appreciation of higher vibrations, which opens up so wonderful a door to its possessor. He claims, or rather he admits—for he is reticent upon the subject—that he has carried this power of perception on from childhood, and his surprise is not so much at what he sees, as at the failure of others to see the same thing. To show that it is not subjective he tells the story that on one occasion while traversing a field he saw a little creature which beckoned eagerly that he should follow. He did so, and presently saw his guide pointing with an air of importance to the ground. There, between the furrows lay a flint arrowhead, which he carried home with him as a souvenir of the adventure.

This gentleman is further distinguished by having that power of attracting animals, even wild animals which some people have, and it may be that this sympathy is the same quality which helps him in getting into touch with fairies. His account of the latter is extraordinarily interesting.

"I should describe them as being between two and three feet in height," says he, "and dressed in brown clothes. The nearest approach I can get to them is to say that they are 'spiritual monkeys.' Their general instinct is to avoid mankind, but they are capable individually of becoming extremely fond of humans—or of *a* human. They are just Peter Pans, children who have never grown up. Speaking generally I should imagine that anyone who has had any truck with the fairies must have obeyed the scriptural injunction to 'become as a little child'—i.e. he or she must be either a Buddha or simple."

Another friend of mine who claimed to have the power of seeing fairies is the late Tom Tyrrell, the famous medium, whose clairvoyance and general psychic gifts were of the strongest character. I cannot easily forget how one evening in a Yorkshire hotel a storm of raps, sounding very much as if someone was cracking their finger and thumb, broke out around his head, and how with his coffee-cup in one hand, he flapped vigorously with the other to warn off his inopportune visitors. In answer to my question about fairies, he says:

"Yes, I do see these little pixies or fairies. I have seen them scores of time. But only in the woods and when I do a little fasting. They are a very real presence to me. What are they? I cannot say. I can never get nearer to the beggars than four or five yards. They seem afraid of me, and they scamper off up the trees like squirrels. I dare say if I were to go in the woods oftener I would perhaps gain their confidence more. They are certainly like human beings only very small, say about twelve or fifteen inches high. I have noticed they are brown in colour, with fairly large heads and standing up ears, out of proportion to the size of their bodies, and bandy legs. I am speaking of what I see. I have never come across any other clairvoyant who has seen them, though I have read that many do so. Probably they have something to do with Nature processes. The males have very short hair, and the females rather long, straight hair."

The idea that these little creatures are occupied in consciously furthering Nature's projects—very much, I suppose, as the bee carries pollen—is repeated by the learned Dr. Vanstone, who combines great knowledge of theory with some considerable experience, though a high development of intellect, is, in spite of Swedenborg's example, a bar to psychic perception. This would show, if it is correct, that we may have to return to the classical conceptions of something in the nature of naiads and fauns and spirits of the trees and groves. Dr. Vanstone, whose experiences are on the borderland between what is objective and what is sensed without being actually seen, writes to me:

"I have been distinctly aware of minute intelligent beings in connection with the evolution of plant forces, particularly in certain localities, for instance in Ecclesbourne Glen. Pond life yields to me the largest and best sense of fairy life, and not the floral world. I may be only clothing my subjective consciousness with unreal objective imaginations, but they are real to me as sentient intelligent beings, able to communicate with us in varying distinctness. I am inclined to think that elemental beings are engaged, like factory hands, in facilitating the operation of Nature's laws."

Another gentleman who claims to have this most remarkable gift is Mr. Tom Charman, in the New Forest, who hunts for fairies as an entomologist would for butterflies. In answer to my inquiries he tells me that the power of vision came to him in childhood, but left him for many years, varying in proportion with his own nearness to nature. According to this seer the creatures are of many sizes, varying from a few inches to several feet. They are male, female, and children. He has not heard them utter sounds but believes that they do so of finer quality than we can hear. They are visible by night as well as by day, and show small lights about the same size as glowworms. They dress in all sorts of ways. Such is Mr. Charman's account.

It is easy, of course, for us who only respond to the more material vibrations, to declare that all these seers are self-deluded or are the victims of some mental twist. It is difficult for them to defend themselves from such a charge. It is, however, to be urged upon the other side that these numerous testimonies come from people who are very solid, practical and successful in the affairs of life. One is a distinguished writer, another an ophthalmic authority, a third a successful professional man, a fourth a lady engaged on public service, and so on. To wave aside the evidence of such people on the ground that it does not correspond with our own experience, is an act of mental arrogance which no wise man will commit.

It is interesting to compare these various contemporary first-hand accounts of the impressions which all these witnesses have received. I have already pointed out that the higher vibration which we associate with hot sunshine, and which we actually seem to see in the shimmer of noon-tide, is associated with many of the episodes. Apart from this it must be admitted that the evidence is on the whole irregular. We have creatures described which range from five inches to two and a half feet. An advocate of the fairies might say that since the tradition has always been that they procreate as human beings do, we are dealing with them in every stage of growth, which accounts for the varying size. It seems to me, however, that a better case could be made out if it were pleaded that there have always been many different races of fairyland, and that samples of these races may greatly differ from each other, and may inhabit varying spots, so that an observer like Mr. Tyrrell for example, may always have seen woodland elves which bear no resemblance to gnomes or goblins. The monkey-like brown-clad creatures of my professional friend, which were over two feet high, compare very closely with the creatures which little Baring-Gould saw climbing on to the horses. In both cases these taller fairies were reported from flat plain-like locations, while the little old man type varies completely from the dancing little feminine elf so beloved by Shakespeare. In the experience of Mr. Turvey and Mr. Lonsdale two different types engaged in different tasks were actually seen at the same moment, the one being bright-coloured dancing elves, while the other were the brown-coloured attendants who guarded over them.

The claim that the fairy rings so often seen in meadow or marshland are caused by the beat of fairy feet is certainly untenable, as they unquestionably come from fungi such as *agaricus gambosus* or *marasmius oveades* which grow from a centre, continually deserting the exhausted ground and spreading to that which is fresh. In this way a complete circle is formed which may be quite small or may be of twelve-foot diameter. These circles appear just as often in woods from the same cause but are smothered over by the decayed leaves among which the fungi grow. But though the fairies most certainly do not produce the rings it might be asserted, and could not be denied, that the rings once formed, whatever their cause, would offer a very charming course for a circular ring-a-ring dance. Certainly from all time these circles have been associated with the gambols of the little people.

After these modern instances one is inclined to read with a little more gravity the accounts which our ancestors gave of these creatures, for however fanciful in parts it still may have had some core of truth. I say "our ancestors," but as a matter of fact there are shepherds on the South Downs to this day who will throw a bit of their bread and cheese over their shoulders at dinner-time for the little folk to consume. All over the United Kingdom, and especially in Wales and in Ireland, the belief is largely held among those folk who are nearest to nature. First of all it was always supposed that they lived within the earth. This was natural enough since a sudden disappearance of a solid body could only be understood in that way. On the whole their description was not grotesque, and fits easily into its place amid the examples already given.

One of the best of the ancient accounts is that of the Rev. R. Kirk who occupied a parish at Monteith on the edge of the Highlands, and wrote a pamphlet called *The Secret Commonwealth* about the year 1680. He had very clear and definite ideas about these little creatures, and he was by no means a visionary but a man of considerable parts, who was chosen afterwards to translate the Bible into Erse. His information about fairies tallies very well with that already quoted. He slips up in imagining that flint arrowheads are indeed "fairy-bolts," but otherwise his contentions agree very well with our modern instances. They have tribes and orders, according to this Scotch clergyman. They eat. They converse in a thin whistling sort of language. They have children, deaths and burials. They are fond of frolic-dancing. They have a regular state and polity with rulers, laws, quarrels and even battles. They are irresponsible creatures, not hostile to the human race unless they have reason to be angry, but even inclined to be helpful, since some of them, the Brownies, are by universal tradition, ready to aid in the household work if the family has known how to engage their affection.

An exactly similar account comes from Ireland, though the little folk seem to have imbibed the spirit of the island to the extent of being more mercurial and irascible. There are many cases on record where they are claimed to have shown their power and to have taken revenge for some slight. In the *Larne Reporter* of March 31, 1866, as quoted in *True Irish Ghost Stories*, there is an account of how a stone which the fairies claimed having been built into a house, the inhabitants were bombarded with stones by invisible assailants by day and night, the missiles hurting no one but causing great annoyance. These stories of stone-throwing are so common, and present such similar well-attested features in cases coming from every part of the world, that they may be accepted as a recognized preternatural phenomenon, whether it be the fairies or some other form of mischievous psychic force which cause the bombardment. The volume already quoted gives another remarkable case where a farmer having built a house upon what was really a fairy right of way between two "raths" or fairy mounds, was exposed to such persecution by noises and other disturbances that his family was at last driven out and had to take refuge in the smaller house which they had previously occupied. This story is narrated by a correspondent from Wexford, who says that he examined the facts himself, examined the deserted house, cross-examined the owner and satisfied himself that there were two raths in the vicinity and that the house was in a deadline between them.

I have particulars of a case in West Sussex which is analogous, and which I have been able to trace to the very lady to whom it happened. This lady desired to make a rock garden, and for this purpose got some large boulders from a field hard by, which had always been known as the pixie stones and built them into her new rockery. One summer evening this lady saw a tiny grey woman sitting on one of the boulders. The little creature slipped away when she knew that she had been observed. Several times she appeared upon the stones. Later the people in the village asked if the stones might be moved back to the field, "as," they said, "they are the pixie stones and if they are moved from their place misfortune will happen in the village." The stones were restored.

But supposing that they actually do exist what *are* these creatures? That is a subject upon which we can only speculate with more or less plausibility. Mr. David Gow, Editor of *Light* and a considerable authority upon psychic matters, had first formed the opinion that they were simply ordinary human spirits seen, as it were, at the wrong end of a clairvoyant telescope, and therefore very minute. A study of the detailed accounts of their varied experience caused him to alter his view and to conclude that they are really life forms which have developed along some separate line of evolution, and which for some morphological reason have assumed human shape in the strange way in which Nature reproduces her types like the figures on the mandrake root, or the frost ferns upon the window.

In a remarkable book, *A Wanderer in the Spirit Lands*, published in 1896, the author, Mr. Farnese, under inspiration, gives an account of many mysteries including that of fairies. What he says fits in very clearly with the facts that have been put forward, and goes beyond them. He says, speaking of elementals,

"Some are in appearance like the gnomes and elves who are said to inhabit mountain caverns. Such, too, are the fairies whom men have seen in lonely and secluded places. Some of these beings are of a very low order of life, almost like the higher order of plants, save that they possess independent motion. Others are very lively and full of grotesque unmeaning tricks . . . As nations advance these lower forms of life die out from the astral plane of that earth's sphere and succeeding generations begin at first to doubt and then to deny that they ever had any existence."

This is one plausible way of explaining the disappearance of the faun, the dryad, the naiad, and all the creatures which are alluded to with such familiarity in the classics of Greece and Rome.

All these evidences as to fairies sink into insignificance compared with the actual photographs which I have published in my *Coming of the Fairies*. These, in the enlarged edition, cover cases from Yorkshire, Devonshire, Canada and Germany, and show varying sizes as already described. Since its publication I have had an excellent one from Sweden. They are not all supported by the same degree of evidence, but each case is strong and all the cases taken together seem to me to be final, unless we are to reconsider altogether our views as to the nature and power of thought-forms. No criticism has for a moment shaken the truth of the original Cottingley pictures. All fresh evidence has tended to confirm it. I refer readers to the book for the full detail, and for the pictures themselves.

Some final paragraphs may be devoted to other forms of elemental life for which there is some evidence, though I admit that it is on a very different level from that which sustains the fairies. In Mrs. Tweedale's *Ghosts I Have Seen,* a book which is far more thrilling than any sensational novel, and which can only be matched by the companion volume, *Phantoms of the Dawn,* will be found several descriptions of fauns, satyrs, and even in one case of a troop of centaurs, which are picturesque and arresting, if not entirely convincing. I know Mrs. Tweedale personally—she is the daughter of one of the famous Chambers brothers of Edinburgh, and I am aware that she is the last woman in the world to exaggerate or trifle with truth. The more remarkable of these elemental stories, however, are given second-hand, so that she cannot be responsible.

There is one curious case which fits into the idea of a satyr-like creature who had by some mischance wandered out of his own vibration and got entangled in matter. I do not venture to say that this is the actual explanation, but I do maintain that the facts appear to be well-attested and that I know no other solution which would fully cover them. They are to be found in a book called *Oddities* published some years ago. It is there shown that on a certain year in the middle of last century, after a slight snow-shower, foot-prints of cleft goat-like feet which were most carefully observed, measured, and even photographed, were found over a hundred miles of ground in Devonshire. These foot-steps had apparently all been made in the one night, and extended right across country over all obstacles, including the Teignmouth estuary, where the marks vanished at one side and re-appeared at the other. They were—I quote from memory—about two inches by one in size. If the facts are correctly given, then an elaborate practical joke carried out by a number of people acting in collusion would be the only alternative to the preternatural one, which I have ventured not to maintain but to suggest as a remote possibility. The case attracted much attention at the time and tracings of the prints are to be found in an old number of the *Illustrated London News*.

One may well ask what connection have fairies and elementals with the essays upon the fate of the human soul which have formed most of this series? The connection is slight and indirect, consisting only in the fact that anything which widens our conceptions of the possible, and shakes us out of our time-rutted lines of thought, helps us to regain our elasticity of mind and thus to be more open to new philosophies. The fairy question is infinitely small and unimportant compared to the question of our own fate and that of the whole human race. The evidence also is very much less impressive though, as I trust I have shown, it is not entirely negligible. These creatures are in any case remote from us and their existence is of little more real importance than that of strange animals or plants. At the same time the perennial mystery, why so many "flowers are born to blush unseen" and why Nature should be so lavish with gifts which human beings cannot use, would be solved if we understood that there were other orders of being which used the same earth and shared its blessings. It is at the lowest an interesting speculation which gives an added charm to the silence of the woods and the wildness of the moorland.

IX

A STRANGE PROPHET

WHEN ONE FINDS that a philosophy is obscure, and when one fails after an earnest effort to get it clear, one may usually conclude that the teacher is also obscure and that the subject has not been clearly thought out. For some time I have endeavoured to get an understanding of Thomas Lake Harris, a mystic about whom there has been the utmost difference of opinion ranging from the Messianic to the diabolical. In my search for truth I have read much that he has written and I have carefully perused his *Life and World Work*, by a devoted follower, Mr. Arthur Cuthbert, who claims to have shared some of the same psychic experiences. I have also studied *Sympneumata*, written by Mrs. Laurence Oliphant and edited by her famous husband. Instead of clearing up obscurities this leaves them more obscure than ever. One earnestly wishes that the husband had expounded the matter, since he could write English, instead of the wife with her interminable and involved sentences which average about two to a page. Finally I read the picture of Harris taken by the novelist, Mrs. Oliphant, who was Laurence's aunt, and who takes a very severe view of the American prophet. At the end of it all I find myself in the same perplexity as ever, and have no sure idea whether I am dealing with a megalomaniac ranter endowed with considerable worldly cunning, or with one who really had a breath of the divine afflatus—whether in fact his philosophy was a cloud of words or whether he had an authentic message.

I am consoled in my indecision, and reassured as to my own judgment when I clearly see that the astute Laurence Oliphant, after twelve years of most intimate association, cannot answer for the real character of his associate. His famous pen-drawing of him in *Masollam* pictures a dual personality with two voices and two ranges of vision, and it ends with the words, "He might be the best or the worst of men." A short sketch of my impressions of this curious man and of his doctrines may be of interest to readers.

Harris was born in Fenny Stratford in Buckinghamshire in 1823, and was five years old when his parents emigrated to the United States, settling in Utica in the north of the State of New York. This region seems to have been to an extraordinary degree the centre of new religions or pseudo-religious impulses from that time onwards. Spiritualism, Mormonism, and, as I believe, Christian Science all had their original springs in this geographical centre. Harris, who was independent of each of these movements, was destined to make a very definite contribution of his own to the general spiritual urge and outreach which was characteristic of the time and place.

His people were narrow Calvinistic Baptists, and at an early age Harris rebelled against their sour doctrines and accepted the wider and more charitable teaching of the Universalists. An officer has told me how upon his inquiring into the religion of a recruit the Sergeant answered, "'E calls 'imself a Christadelphian, but to my mind 'e's little better than an 'eathen." Probably this was the view taken of the Universalists in those days of dogma. It was the nature of Harris to reject all dogmas, until he came to put forward some of his own. He was twenty years of age when he chanted his religion, and he has left it on record that his dead mother appeared to him at that time and said, "My dear child, my poor child, you must all remember that God is the father of all men and that all mankind are your brothers."

He seems to have been a most eloquent preacher and soon won a considerable name, but the rather vague tenets of his new creed made him crave for something in the nature of concrete proof. Some chance of this was offered at this period by the use of Spiritualism, and in order to get clearer views upon the subject Harris paid a visit to Andrew Jackson Davis, who after some experiences as a hypnotic subject had finally become an inspired medium. The meeting and intercourse of these two men was certainly a notable event, for in their different ways they were both remarkable characters, and each has a niche of his own in religious history. Harris was twenty-four at the time and Davis twenty, two most singular youths. Davis converted Harris to the idea of spirit intercourse and for some years Harris was an enthusiastic preacher and leader. Davis, however, had some peculiar amatory adventures, depicted in his *Magic Staff*, and Harris, who professed a deeper regard for the marriage vow, was disillusioned and turned as violent an opponent as he had been a friend of the Spiritualistic movement. His attitude seems to have been supremely illogical, for the ill-doings, granting that they exist, of any member of a philosophy cannot alter the facts upon which the philosophy is founded. It would be as reasonable for an inquirer to discard Christianity in order to show disapproval of Judas. The fact remains, however, that Harris was seen no more on Spiritualistic platforms and that his voice was raised against all that he had supported. To anyone who is acquainted with the true tenets of this cult it must be obvious that he had never grasped their meaning and seemed to consider that an artificial hypnotism was essential to mediumship. His objections are mostly founded upon the supposition that one comes in contact with evil spirits. One may find plenty of evil spirits in the flesh, but one chooses one's company and one finds that it is not difficult to come into contact with the higher ones as well. This great fact Harris ignored and from that moment his life took a turn of its own, and he lost touch with any philosophy which is capable of clear expression, though it influenced strongly a small circle of followers.

He still ministered to a considerable church in New York, the congregation of which, including Horace Greeley, must have been sorely exercised in endeavouring to keep pace with, or to understand, the spiritual gyrations of their pastor. It was called the Independent Christian Church and was still on universalist lines. He narrates that addresses which he delivered there came to him by what Spiritualists now call automatic writing, and that the purpose and ultimate effect of them was the redemption of destitute children—an admission which one would have supposed must modify his condemnation of spirit intercourse. At this period he was one of those who founded a colony called the Mountain Cave Association, which was dissolved after a short and not too honourable existence. It was this first experiment in communal life which no doubt suggested the larger developments to come.

It was at this time, about 1850, that Harris received according to his own account a direct revelation from a majestic angel man who turned his thoughts into a special channel. This tale of the direct apparition occurs in Swedenborg's first vision, in Smith's revelation of Mormonism, and in Davis's account of his experience in the hills near Poughkeepsie. Considering the recent close association with the latter seer, it is not entirely impossible that Harris's vision may have been subconsciously suggested by what he had heard of the apparition seen by Davis. The first fruits of the new departure were a long poem of 6,000 lines which was completed in the extraordinary time of twenty-seven working hours, scattered over fourteen days. It may be said once for all that Harris in this and many subsequent poems, which were so copious that it is doubtful if any writer has ever composed so much, showed himself to be a true poet of a high order. Laurence Oliphant put him at the very top, and without being able to go so far as that, I should say that he stood very high. There are times when in his strong simplicity of phrase he reminds one of Blake, and there are times when his high spirituality touches the edge of Shelley. As an example of the former I would take:

"Nine months I lay in a Lady's womb,
She folded me all in her laughing bloom,
She hallowed me while I filled and fed
From the nectar-walls of her mother head."

As to the latter almost any page from his longer poems would illustrate my meaning.

Lyrical speech seems to have been his natural expression, which accounts for a certain rhythm and majesty in his addresses. A lady who knew him at that period wrote of him:

"When in Utica he would come to my sitting-room of an evening and sitting down on a rather high chair—one which allowed him to swing his feet rhythmically, he would compose poetry by the mile—exquisite thoughts, exquisitely worded. My memories of those quiet hours are very beautiful. There was nothing impressive about his person then; he was too thin, really lank, but his eyes were very full of thought and his voice had a rare charm. His poetic utterances were to me like views of sunset and sunrise, which we enjoy internally but which we cannot remember."

This last sentence seems to me to be very good criticism, well observed and clearly expressed. The reason seems to be that it is all too transcendental and ethereal. When Tennyson discusses the deeper things of life there are constant touches which bring one back to human experience. Harris is off the ground all the time. There is no anchor by which one may attach him to the current life of man. Hence one reads, as the lady says, with admiration for the limpid verse and the lofty thought, and yet at the end there is little which has remained as part of one's own mental storehouse.

And now the time had come when Harris had to strike out a path of his own into the unknown, and a very vague and difficult path it is for anyone else to indicate—far less to follow. There is an objective side to it and there is a theoretical or dogmatic side. The objective side of this system lay in the assertion that by some system of breathing certain psychic results may be obtained, and the mind elucidated as to things divine. It is to be presupposed that such exercises of the diaphragm or solar plexus—for those are indicated as being physically involved—are concomitant with mental and spiritual efforts, otherwise the matter would be no more a sign of progress than results to be obtained by standing upon one's head. On the other hand, one would suppose that if the mental and spiritual effort had been made the advance would be automatic and independent of physical exertions. However, the theory is as I have stated, and there are found other witnesses, such as Mr. Cuthbert, who assert that they have themselves gone through the early stages of illumination as produced in this fashion. There are said to be seven stages in this advance by breath, each of them to be obtained by long and apparently painful effort. No one save Harris himself had ever attained the seventh, though all his followers, including his successive wives, three in number, were on various rungs of the ladder. The fact that Harris himself was supposed to have passed through the whole seven degrees was the basis for claims which must startle if not convince the general public, since it was seriously stated that the Christ was the only person who had ever done so much. The process, however, seems to have escaped the notice of the apostles, since it is mentioned in no gospel, and Paul, who gave so full a list of the spiritual gifts, has said nothing on the subject.

At the same time it is not to be denied that there is a considerable body of evidence that by a certain control of the breath some exalted mental condition can be obtained. In Swedenborg's case the more shallow his breathing the more spiritual his frame of mind. Cataleptics appear not to breathe at all, and are from time to time buried alive in consequence, but the condition seems to go with remarkable enfranchisement of the spirit. The Hindoos have reduced it to a system and claim similar results. I can remember in Canterbury, New Zealand, meeting some people who practised it; and who assured me that I was not without danger, as the excursion of the soul leaves an empty house behind, which may attract a parasitic tenant. However that may be, Harris's general claim meets with some support, though I know no proof that any high spirituality is necessarily associated with what would rather seem to be a curious physiological experiment. This breathing phenomenon is, so far as I know, the only objective part of Harris's philosophy.

We come, therefore, to its dogmatic side, which consists in the assertion of the dual sex in everyone, including the Creator. Bi-une is the word which covers the philosophy. So far is it pushed that even a name is given to this second personality, so that the Lady Jessa is associated with the Lord Jesus, and Harris himself is closely intertwined with the Lady Lily to the not unnatural confusion of his earthly wives. So high is the Lady Lily that the whole celestial region after death is named Lilistan. This dual internal mating is supposed to do away with the coarser processes of nature and to free mankind from the lustful morass in which he is accused of wallowing, but as Harris had not only wives but also children, it would appear that the higher path was not all-sufficing.

In that most incomprehensible book, *Sympneumata*, which might well be translated into English, there is a disquisition upon the bi-une gods of old, in which Isis and Osiris, Hathor and Ra, Bel and Bilit, with many others are duly paired. Considering the practical results of these old systems one would think that their teachings are rather to be avoided than followed. What is to be gained, or how would human life be elevated by our following hermaphroditic divinities? So far as the case is applicable to human beings it has, of course, that amount of obvious truth that a man does reproduce many of the qualities of his mother, and a girl may do the same by the father, and so each sex may manifest its presence in the composite result. There are also anatomical facts which correspond with the psychological unison. But when this is said one cannot see that much remains. The discussion of sex in connection with the Deity seems incongruous and repulsive, nor does Harris ever give any clear reason why such strange dogmas should be given to a world which is already sick of unproved assertions and struggling hard to escape from wild faiths into a region of concrete proof. Had Harris ever really understood Spiritualism he would have realized that this concrete proof for which the whole intellect of the human race is yearning, may well be found in that direction.

There were some other peculiar beliefs in the Harris cosmogony. One was that the planets were inhabited by spirits, some superior and some inferior to those upon earth. There was a reaction between these beings and ourselves. Another was that fairies, or as he preferred to call them, fays, played a very important part in the development of man's spirit. That such creatures exist and that they play some lowly part in nature is held by many and is supported by evidence which will bear examination, but for the ambitious spiritual rôle here assigned to them there is no evidence at all, unless we extend the term "fay" to include those higher entities or angels who may reasonably be supposed to have some guiding influence in our lives.

Apart from obscure doctrines there was one side of the Harris system with which many of us would cordially agree. It was that we would do well to get back to the simple life. He founded successive communities for this alleged purpose, and the system adopted was called "The Use." The first colony was assembled in a farm-house at Wassiac in 1861. In 1863 it moved to America, where it centred round a mill and a bank. In the latter institution Mr. Harris, the president, is depicted as spending much of his time. "Here the people come on business together and others would sit down and smoke and talk over their affairs and general politics, while the President himself would be frequently occupying one of the chairs in the midst of them and entering into full sympathy with them in a perfectly natural, ordinary, neighbourly fashion." It is a pleasant picture which Mr. Cuthbert draws, but somehow one wishes it was not a bank.

Just about this time a most amazing thing happened. The prophet had gone with his wife to England for the purpose of securing the publication of some of his works. While there he gave some lectures or sermons at the Steinway Hall. His ornate and rather inflated style of eloquence, which like his poetry is limpid and vaguely beautiful, attracted audiences, among whom was Lady Oliphant, the mother of the famous writer and diplomatist, one of the most rising men in England. She brought her son to hear the further lectures, and the views of the prophet struck some sympathetic mystic chord in their own bosoms. The idea of the simple community life with its dreamy religious background appealed strongly to natures which were weary of the empty ways of fashion and unsatisfied by the unreasonable dogmas of the churches. They liquidated their business affairs, left their homes and threw in their lot with the American community. This access of fresh strength and money enabled the colonists to move to Brocton near Buffalo, where some large farms were taken and the whole project took on a more ambitious aspect.

Those who wish to see a critical and adverse view of the matter will find it in Mrs. Oliphant's life of her famous nephew. One can well understand that it was galling to the pride of a grand old Scottish family that their finest product should come under the complete sway of what seemed to them to be a very dubious American adventurer. How complete that sway was may be judged from the fact that the next ten or twelve years of Laurence Oliphant's life were spent in menial agricultural tasks, which included the selling of strawberries at the railway station to the passengers in the trains. There is, we must admit, something of beauty and of sanctity in this utilitarian age, that a man should humble himself for spiritual ends, and yet when one considers the exceptional gifts with which this particular man had been endowed, one doubts whether anything could excuse the diversion of his energies into a channel so useless to the world. Such was the complete subservience of the young Scot that he had with difficulty to get leave of absence from Brocton in order to act as war correspondent in the Franco-German war. Even more incredible, he had to ask leave to marry, and after the marriage was separated for a long time from his wife by orders of the autocratic prophet. It is amazing how any man of spirit could submit to such a position, and no adequate explanation of it has ever been given. It would seem that Harris held a fairly substantial hostage for Oliphant's behaviour in the fact that a large part of the latter's fortune was locked up in the Brocton property, which, however, was not held in the name of Harris but in that of the community at large. Oliphant was not the only person of distinction in the little company, for there were several Japanese who had come presumably on his recommendation, as he had made many friends in that nation during his diplomatic visit to their country. One of these Japanese afterwards became Ambassador at London and a second Ambassador at Paris, so that either the personality or the teaching of Harris must have had some very real attraction for intelligent followers.

The prophet, in spite of his seven stages of breathing and the agonies of spirit or of body which those stages represented, seems to have had a very human side in his complex personality. He enjoyed the good things of life, including a cigar and a glass of wine, while the heartiness of his laughter was proverbial. He had an excellent head for commercial affairs and he built a second bank, a hotel, a general store, a railway restaurant, and many other amenities in connection with his colony. Finally, finding a larger and more profitable field available, he started a considerable vineyard at Fountain Grove in the extreme south of California, which no doubt still produces the raisins by which so many private stills mitigate the austerities of Prohibition. One would have a fuller sympathy with these activities if they were not mixed up with strange religious jargon, so that it was actually claimed that the wine from the vineyards contained within it "a divine-natural vital substance."

In the midst of his worldly work Harris found time to write a great deal both of verse and of prose. Of the former I have already given my opinion. I cannot speak so favourably of the prose. Mr. Cuthbert in his *Life and Work* devotes some seventy pages to quotations from what he calls "this great book," which was afterwards published as *The New Republic* and *God's Breath in Man*. There may be an esoteric meaning to it all which gives it a special value to his followers, but on the face of it to an ordinary critic it would appear to be turgid stuff with no trace of greatness, and with a considerable tendency to both blasphemy and obscenity. I will confess that I am influenced in my judgment of Harris by this work, and that after reading it I cannot doubt that the man who wrote it had at that time an utterly unbalanced mind, and that as a guide he could only lead one to disaster. The man's life was many-sided, however, and, as I have tried to show, there were other aspects of it and other literary productions which were less open to criticism.

The Laurence Oliphant episode came to an end after some twelve years of subjection. There is no record how the rift began, but both the writer and his mother had gradually become disillusioned. It can hardly be imagined that such writings as those alluded to above could fail to repel educated and sensitive minds. They may have found the worldly and successful prophet a very different person to the spiritual enthusiast who had originally led them into the wilderness. The parting was by no means friendly. Oliphant took legal processes in order to recover some portion of his property, while Harris in return tried to put Oliphant into a lunatic asylum. Eventually some part of the money was recovered, and Oliphant moved away on his curious orbit, winding up at El Harja in Syria, where he spent his latter years. The fact that he allowed his wife to publish *Sympneumata* and that the book is adorned by many scraps of verse which, though unacknowledged by the authoress, are clearly from the pen of Harris, show that in some respects his views about the prophet had not been changed.

There is little more to record of Harris, who dwelt for the most part on his California estate, save that in his seventieth year he announced that he had passed his final stage of breathing, and had thus reached what was claimed to be a unique position among mankind. He announced the event in the *Sonoma Democrat*, and his statement is more definite than most of the cloud of words which obscure the subject. He wrote:

"For the last two or three years I have been secluded most of the time in my mountain retreat, working to the final solutions of the problems that opened in my discoveries of forty years ago. The final problem that faced me during these years was . . . how, without passing through physical disease, shall man practically embody and realize the resurrection. . . . The alternative was success or dissolution. Success came as suddenly and pleasantly as when a deep-laden, storm-tossed ship glides over the harbour-bar from the raging outside sea and swings at ease in a landlocked haven. I have passed through December. I am in Maytime. . . . No more an old man of over seventy but now renewed in more than the physical and mental powers of the early prime, my retirement is at an end. . . . I leave the disposition of my honour to the slow but finally just unveilings of coming time. Each hour of my days must be devoted to labour of necessity and beneficence."

These brave words should have been the cry of the centenarian. It was not destined to be. It was not, however, until he had reached the ripe but not extraordinary age of eighty-three that Thomas Lake Harris took leave of his Californian vineyard and journeyed on to Lilistan or whatever other sphere of the coming world he had earned by his strange mixed career. He has certainly left behind him one of the most curious personal and religious problems with which I am acquainted.

X
A LONDON GHOST

For some days the papers had contained accounts of a haunted house within a few hundred yards of Piccadilly Circus, which had aroused the interest of the public.

The allegations, founded on the actual experiences of residents, were, that in the lower room of this building there was a perceptible and evil psychic atmosphere, that raps were heard, that a luminous ray was seen on the stair, and that a figure of an elderly man with an evil face had several times been seen by a young woman who was employed professionally on the premises.

It was to test this matter that a few of us assembled on the night of May 28th, 1924, reaching the house at eleven o'clock. It was in the theatre neighbourhood, and it was a curious change from the streets, which were crowded with the returning pleasure-seekers, to the absolute silence of the sinister old house which stands in a by-street.

Our party consisted of the young woman already quoted, whom I will call the clairvoyante, the secretary of the business, a young Dutch artist who claimed also to have psychic vision, Mr. Horace Leaf, who is a strong medium, a Wimpole Street physician, the Rev. Vale Owen, and myself.

As I had organized the expedition I took it on myself to guard the party against practical jokers. All doors were locked and a piece of twine was tied across the only staircase which led down to the lower room.

In this lower room we assembled, and at 11:30, having grouped ourselves round a table so that we might be in a position to obtain table messages, we turned out the lights. No sound at all reached us from the street, and we sat quietly awaiting events, chatting occasionally among ourselves, as experience has shown that sound vibrations are helpful in psychic phenomena.

At first the darkness had seemed absolute. Gradually, however, we were able to discern a dim light on the stair. It had a spectral effect, but we were all in agreement that it was caused by a reflection from the glass roof of the building, and that it was our own vision, growing gradually used to the conditions, which had caused it to develop.

We were not aware of any particular psychic atmosphere. There were a few distant taps, or cracks, but not more than is usual in an old house in the silence of the night-time.

Our hands were all on the table, which occasionally thrilled and shook, but gave no pronounced movement. We had begun to think that our results might be entirely negative when the clairvoyante on my left whispered in an agitated voice:

"I see him. He is there. He is standing on the stair looking down at us."

"An elderly man, bearded, with rather slit eyes and a cunning expression," was her description of the apparition. It was corroborated by the Dutchman. I could see the faint luminosity which marked the line of the stairs, but nothing more.

I do not, however, possess any psychic perceptions. The two seers reported that the man had descended a little, and the clairvoyante showed signs of considerable emotion.

We spoke, begging the unseen figure to approach us and to tell us how we could assist it. A moment later the two seers agreed that it was no longer on the stair.

In a minute the table began to move. It rose and fell in a steady rhythm. My experience of table-sittings, which is a large one, has shown me that undeveloped spirits always make violent and irregular—often circular—movements, and that steady movement is a sign of a deliberate, thoughtful control.

We were reassured, therefore, as regards the nature of our invisible visitant. Having explained the code, the dialogue between us ran thus, the answers coming clear-cut and swift.

"Are you a spirit?"—"Yes."

"A man?"—"Yes."

"Are you the spirit who has haunted this room?"—"Yes."

"Have you a reason for haunting it?"—"Yes."

"Is it money that troubles you?"—"No."

"Papers?"—"No."

"Remorse for deeds done?"—"Yes."

I then explained to the spirit the conditions under which he lived, and the need to turn his thoughts away from worldly matters, which retarded spiritual progress. I begged him to cease to annoy innocent people, and I told him that he could only work out his own salvation by adapting his mind to the new conditions, by being unselfish, and by striving for higher things.

I said that we would pray for him, and Mr. Vale Owen, there and then, offered up a beautiful prayer that this, our unhappy brother, might be eased and helped. I then asked if he had heard and understood.

"Yes," was the reply.

Had it affected his attitude of mind? Some hesitation, and then "No." Clearly he was a man of resolute character, not easily to be influenced.

I then said that we would take any message from him, and would like first of all to know his earth name. With that object I gave him the alphabet slowly, asking him to move the table sharply on the right letter. The following letters came out: L-E-N-A-N.

"Is that right?" I asked.—"No," was the reply.

"Is L E N right?"—"Yes."

"Should the next letter be I?"—"Yes."

"Is Lenin the name?"—"Yes."

"Are you Lenin the Russian leader?"—"Yes."

All our company protested that this man's name was not in the minds of anyone. Certainly it was, up to the last moment, unexpected by me.

"Could you spell something in Russian?" was the next question.— "Yes," was the answer.

Some lingual tests were then given, but I found it hard to follow them, for spelling out with the alphabet is hard work even in one's own tongue. The Dutch artist addressed the Intelligence in several languages, and received correct "Yes" or "No" answers, which showed comprehension.

"Have you a message for us?" I then asked.

"Yes," was the reply.

"Then I will give you the alphabet."

It was slow work, but this was the queer sentence which finally was hammered out:

"Artists must rouse selfish nations."

I thought that by "artists" he was using a short cut to express the idea of all men of intelligence and imagination.

We asked if this was the whole message, and were told that it was not. As the alphabet procedure was so slow and clumsy, Mr. Horace Leaf suggested that we should put the table aside, sit in a circle, and invite the spirit to control one or other of us.

Both Mr. Leaf and the artist volunteered to be the subjects of the experiment. We rearranged ourselves, therefore, and sang "Lead, kindly light," for the sake of harmony and vibration.

Suddenly, in the pitch darkness, a strange voice broke in on a low, level, clear tone. It was Mr. Leaf's own personal guide.

"There is a spirit here who wishes to speak. He is a strong spirit. No, I would not say that he is an evil spirit. His aura is not evil. Yes, he is foreign. I could not say more than that." The voice died away once more.

Presently we heard gasps and short cries of pain. The spirit was endeavouring to possess Mr. Leaf. It was clearly ignorant of psychic things, and did not know how to set about it. What it really did was to produce violent muscular contractions.

Mr. Owen on one side and the doctor on the other had all they could do to hold his twisting, convulsed arms. Then, with a long sigh, he came back to consciousness. The attempt had been a failure—and a painful one.

We were at a loss now how to proceed, and the table was reintroduced while the Dutchman took my place as questioner.

"The spirit is laughing," said the clairvoyante. She had on other occasions observed this sneering laugh.

There is something slightly evidential here, for she had no recollection of Lenin's face as it was in life, but it may be recalled that he had a perpetual set contraction of his lips which gave the impression of a broad smile, which was belied by his serious eyes.

From our new attempts we gathered that the rest of the message was an expression of the desire that Russia and Britain should be friends, with the warning that unless they could come to terms they would drift into war, in which Russia would be very strong.

Such was the whole message. Immediately it was given the table turned dead, and we could obtain no further sign of intelligence. The clairvoyante reported the figure as sitting on the stairs for a time and then passing on.

So ended our curious experience in the old house in mid-London. It cannot be said that there was anything objective to which the senses of all of us could testify. On the other hand, it is certain that we were all in earnest, that there was no pressure on the table, that the messages were clear, and that the whole course of events was consistent.

In answer to a question the Intelligence said that he had lived in London and that he had known these premises, though he had never actually lodged there. It may be added that it is a place frequented by foreign artists, with Russians among them, and that Lenin during his stay in London might well have been there.

Mr. Vale Owen's feeling was that the visitor took it for granted that we were artists also, and that in his message "artists" is in the vocative. If he were mistaken about our vocation it would prove that he was indeed external to ourselves. It was an appeal to us to rouse nations out of their selfishness—an appeal which could hardly come from an evil spirit.

I am not sure of the doctor's conclusions, but I am convinced that everyone else in the company was convinced that we were in touch with a real entity, with a real message, and it is our hope that, the message being delivered, the ghost of mid-London will be heard of no more.

Deception from the other side is an alternative and possible hypothesis, but we were all impressed by the extreme earnestness of this intelligence, and equally earnest were our own invocations to his honesty.

XI

THE HALF-WAY HOUSE
OF MATTER

IN HIS RECENT WORK, *Life After Death*, the late Professor Hyslop, who was formerly Professor of Logic at Columbia University and became the chief American authority upon matters psychic, has a sentence which sounds rather intolerant. It runs: "Any man who does not accept the existence of discarnate spirits and the proof of it is either ignorant or a moral coward." The words are literally true, and yet what removes the sting is that there is really no great reproach up to now in being ignorant. Much of the information is very recent and is contained in works which have not been translated and which are expensive and difficult to get. It is true that we have Crawford's splendid work at Belfast and Crookes's researches of fifty years ago, but both of these needed the corroboration and elucidation of the continental observers to bring out their full meaning. I will try in this article to show any man who is capable of adapting his mind to fresh facts that this tremendous issue is no longer a fair subject for debate, but has been definitely settled up to a certain point—a point which gives us a solid basis for the researches of the future. All recent discoveries, whether they be of aviation, wireless telegraphy, or other material novelties, are insignificant beside a development which shows us a new form of matter, with unheard-of properties, lying latent in all probability within each of us. By a strange paradox the searchers after spirit have come to know more about matter, and its extraordinary possibilities, than any materialist has learned.

It should first be stated that the development of psychic phenomena was a gradual one, and that it was some years after the Hydesville outbreak before actual materializations of spirit were reported. During the 'sixties and 'seventies they became more common, lending themselves greatly to fraud, as people had little critical knowledge as yet and darkness was a physical necessity for their production. Apart from the frauds, however, discriminating observers were aware that there was a large residuum of cases which were undoubtedly genuine. In examining and reporting these cases the witnesses averred that certain people, whom they called "materializing mediums," had the strange physical gift that they could put forth from their bodies a viscous, gelatinous substance which appeared to differ from every known form of matter in that it could solidify and be used for material purposes, and yet could be re-absorbed, leaving absolutely no trace even upon the clothes which it had traversed in leaving the body. This substance was actually touched by some enterprising investigators, who reported that it was elastic and appeared to be sensitive, as though it was really an organic extrusion from the medium's body. These views were naturally much ridiculed by scientific men, who disposed of them easily upon anatomical and also on general physical grounds. Later investigation has, however, shown, as I hope to demonstrate in this article, that in this as in other matters the early Spiritualists were the pioneers of truth, and that they had come upon the most singular manifestation of matter with which we have any acquaintance—a form which might almost be called a half-way house to Spirit.

Mme. Alexandre-Bisson, a French lady with a scientific bent, set herself in the year 1909 to study this phenomenon, having as her subject a woman named Eva, who had the power of forming this substance, which Charles Richet, the great French physiologist, has named ectoplasm. She had as collaborator a German doctor, Schrenck-Notzing, who afterwards collected the notes of the sittings and had them published in French with Mme. Bisson's name appended, under the title *Les Phénomènes dits de Materialization*. A single sentence from the preface gives the gist of the book. He says:

"We have very often been able to establish that, by an unknown biological process, there comes from the body of the medium a material, at first semi-fluid, which possesses some of the properties of a living substance, notably that of the power of change, of movement, and of the assumption of definite forms."

He adds: "One might doubt the truth of these facts if they had not been verified hundreds of times in the course of laborious tests under varied and very strict conditions." Could there be a more complete vindication of those early Spiritualists who for two generations bore with patience the ridicule of the world? Schrenck-Notzing ends his dignified preface by exhorting his fellow-worker to take heart.

"Do not allow yourself to be discouraged in your efforts to open a new domain for science, either by foolish attacks, by cowardly calumnies, by the misrepresentation of facts, by the malevolent, or by any other sort of intimidation. Advance always along the path that you have opened, thinking of the words of Faraday, 'Nothing is too amazing to be true'."

The methods of these wonderful experiments were as follows: All conceivable precautions were taken against fraud. Eva, the medium, seems, so far as one can trace her career, to have been no worse if she was no better than her fellows. A fierce controversy had raged round a previous series of experiments with her conducted in 1906 in Algiers, but Charles Richet and other observers who were present had found no flaw in them. However, nothing was left to chance. The key of the séance room was kept in Mme. Bisson's own pocket. Eva was compelled to change into a special dress when in that room, undressing again when she emerged. She submitted to physical examinations at the hands of doctors. The illumination of the room was gradually increased until six strong, red, electric lamps were at work—red being, as in photography, the one bearable colour. Most important of all, a number of cameras, eight in the last period, were directed upon the medium from all angles, and these were operated by flashlight without warning, so that no motion upon her part could be unobserved. Altogether two hundred and one photographs were taken and reprinted in the book. The sittings lasted with intervals for four years, and were witnessed not only by Mme. Bisson and the German doctor, but by a number of scientific observers whose names are given.

The results are, in my opinion, among the most notable of any investigation which has ever been recorded. It was testified by witnesses, and shown by the photographs, that there oozed from the medium's mucous membranes, and occasionally from her skin, this extraordinary gelatinous material. The pictures are strange and repulsive, but many of Nature's processes seem so in our eyes. You can see this streaky, viscous stuff hanging like icicles from the chin, dripping down on to the body and forming a white apron, or projecting in shapeless lumps from the orifices of the face. When touched, or when undue light came upon it, it writhed back into the body as swiftly and stealthily as the tentacles of a hidden octopus. If seized and pinched, the medium cried aloud. It would protrude through clothes and vanish again, leaving hardly any trace upon them. With the assent of the medium, a small piece was amputated. It dissolved in the box in which it was placed as snow would have done, leaving moisture and some large cells which might have come from a fungus. The microscope also disclosed epithelial cells from the mucous membrane in which the stuff seemed to originate.

It should be explained that the usual Spiritualistic habit of putting the medium into a confined space formed by curtains was followed. This is called the cabinet. She sat therein upon a chair, but her hands always protruded, as an additional safeguard against fraud. The object of the cabinet is that some condensation of material, which we can best describe perhaps as a heavy vapour, is necessary before you get the ectoplasm. The methods call for clearer scientific definition, but in practice it is found that anything which will make an enclosed space and conserve force is of great importance. Those curious, curving draperies which are seen round spirit photographs are the means which the control upon the other side adopts for this end, and I have often observed that the spirit lights at a séance are hooded and flanked by some fine, filmy material for the same reason.

The production of this strange ectoplasm is enough in itself to make such experiments revolutionary and epoch-making, but what follows is far stranger, and will answer the question in every reader's mind, "What has all this to do with spirits?" You must know, then, utterly incredible as it may appear, that this substance, after forming, begins in the case of some mediums, Eva being one, to curdle into definite shapes, and those shapes are human limbs and human faces, seen at first in two dimensions upon the flat, and then moulding themselves at the edges until they become detached and complete. Very many of the photographs exhibit these strange phantoms, which are often much smaller than life. Some of these faces may represent thought-forms from the brain of Eva taking visible form, and some rough resemblance has been traced between some of them and pictures which she may have seen and stored in the memory. One, for example, looks like an extremely rakish President Wilson with a moustache, while another resembles a ferocious rendering of M. Poincaré. One of them shows the word "Miroir" printed over the head of the medium, which some critics have claimed as showing that she had smuggled in the journal of that name, though what the object of such a proceeding could be has not been explained. Her own explanation was that the controlling forces had in some way, possibly by apport, brought in the word in order to convey the idea that these faces and figures are not their real selves, but their selves as seen in a mirror.

Even now the reader may see no obvious connection with Spiritualism, but the next stage takes us all the way. When Eva is at her best, and it occurs only at long intervals and at some cost to her own health, there forms a complete figure; this figure is moulded to resemble some deceased person, the cord which binds it to the medium is loosened, a personality which either is or pretends to be that of the dead takes possession of it, and the breath of life is breathed into the image so that it moves and talks and expresses the emotions of the spirit within. The last word of the Bisson record is: "Since these séances and on numerous occasions the entire phantom has shown itself, it has come out of the cabinet, has begun to speak, and has reached Mme. Bisson, whom it has embraced on the cheek. The sound of the kiss was audible." Was there ever a stranger finale of a scientific investigation? It may serve to illustrate how impossible it is for even the cleverest of materialists to find any explanation of such facts which are consistent with his theories, that the only one which Mr. Joseph MacCabe, in his public debate with me, could put forward was that it was a case of the regurgitation of food! He seemed to me unaware that a close-meshed veil was worn over the medium's face in some of the experiments without in the least hampering the flow of the ectoplasm.

These results, though checked in all possible ways, were none the less so amazing that the inquirer had a right to suspend judgment until they are confirmed. But this has been fully done. Dr. Schrenck-Notzing returned to Munich and there he was fortunate enough to find another medium, a Polish lady, who possessed the faculty of materialization. With her he conducted a series of experiments which he has recorded in his book, *Materialization-phénomène*. Working with Stanislawa, the Polish medium, and adopting the same strict methods as with Eva, he produced exactly the same results. His book overlaps that of Mme. Bisson, since he gives an account of the Paris experiments, but the most important part is the corroboration furnished by his check experiments in the summer of 1912 in Munich. The various photographs of the ectoplasm so far as they go are hardly to be distinguished from those already taken, so that any theory of elaborate fraud upon the part of Eva postulates the same fraud on the part of Stanislawa. Many German observers checked the sittings. In his thorough Teutonic fashion Schrenck-Notzing goes deeper into the matter than Mme. Bisson. He obtained hair from one of the materialized forms and compared it microscopically with hair from Eva (this incident occurred in the French series), showing by several tests that it could not be from the same person. He gave also the chemical result of an examination of a small portion of ectoplasm, which burned to an ash, leaving a smell as of horn. Chloride of soda (common salt) and phosphate of calcium were amongst the constituents. Finally, he actually obtained a cinematograph record of the ectoplasm pouring from the mouth of the medium. Part of this is reproduced in his book.

It should be explained that though the medium was in a trance during these experiments she was by no means inanimate. A separate personality seemed to possess her, which might be explained as one of her own secondary individualities, or as an actual obsession from outside. This personality was in the habit of alluding with some severity to the medium, telling Mme. Bisson that she needed discipline and had to be kept up to her work. Occasionally this person showed signs of clairvoyance, explaining correctly, for example, what was amiss with an electric fitting when it failed to work. A running accompaniment of groans and protests from Eva's body seems to have been a mere animal outcry apart from intelligence.

One observation of the German scientist is worth noting, as it suggests that great injustice may have been done in the past. He is commenting upon a case where Eva was entirely covered by a fantastic helmeted garment of ectoplasm and stood up from her chair. He says:

"This case is interesting because it throws a light upon the state of so-called transfiguration, which in the sense used by the Spiritualists means that a medium plays the part of the spirit, since he is clad with materialized stuff and seeks to imitate the character of the person concerned. This transition stage is to be found in the career of nearly all materialization mediums. Literature records a number of exposures of such mediums acting the part of spirits, like the medium Bastian before Crown Prince Rudolph, Crookes's medium Miss Cook, Mme. Esperance, and others. In all these cases people seized the medium, but the stuff used for the disguise vanished instantly and could not afterwards be traced."

Spiritualists have been slow in advancing this plea, lest it seem to exonerate real fraud, but this conclusion from a man of science in an independent position should be set on record lest indiscriminate disgrace should fall upon the human hyena with his material muslin and the true medium, in trance clad in ectoplasmic drapery.

These separate results of the German and the French investigators would seem final to any reasonable mind, but they are corroborated once again by the shorter research of the late Dr. Geley, of Paris, who held a series of sittings with Eva, summoning a hundred men of science to witness one or other of them. So strict were his tests that he winds up his account in *Physiologie Supernormale* with the words: "I will not merely say that there is no fraud, I will say that there has not been the possibility of fraud." Again he walked the old path and found the same results, save that the phantasms in his experiments took the form of female faces, sometimes beautiful and, as he assures me, unknown to him. They may be thought-forms from Eva, for in none of his recorded results did he get an absolute living entity. There was enough, however, to cause Dr. Geley to say: "What we have seen kills materialism. There is no longer any room for it in the world." By this he means, of course, the old-fashioned materialism of Victorian days, by which thought was a result of matter. All the new evidence points to matter being the result of thought. It is only when you ask, "Whose thought?" that you get upon debatable ground. "They had great beauty and a remarkable appearance of life," says Dr. Geley, though they came as miniatures as well as full size.

Once again, then, Mme. Bisson is corroborated, and we have three separate investigators and two separate mediums giving identical results. Is it not a perfect insanity of incredulity to wave these things aside because they will not fit into our present philosophies? Surely it is evident that the time has come when the philosophies must be expanded to receive them.

Now, having thoroughly got it into our heads that it is possible for a person to evolve very singular stuff with a tendency to form human frames which seem for a time to be tenanted by independent intelligence, let us hark back and apply the knowledge to cases which were proved but not understood before these wonderful experiments. At once the instance of Crookes and Florrie Cook in 1873 springs to the front. In this classic case, as is well known, the celebrated chemist for three years experimented with this young medium, who put herself at his disposal in order to clear herself of a charge of personation made against her. It may well have been an example of transfiguration, as may some other alleged cases which were said to have occurred in later years when she was Mrs. Corner. Crookes exonerated her completely as the result of his research. She was shut up in the dark time and again in his small study. Then, after an hour or so, there would emerge into the adjoining laboratory an entirely different woman, who moved, spoke, and gave her name as Katie King, saying that she was a spirit who had lived in the reign of Charles II, and was now permitted for a brief visit to inhabit the body moulded from Miss Cook, who could be heard, and on certain occasions seen, in the adjoining room. Naturally the obvious criticism was made that this *was* Miss Cook masquerading as a phantom, but the first objection to such a theory was that it makes Professor Crookes out to be either a lunatic or a deliberate liar. No one but a lunatic could be so deceived, and no one but a liar could declare that the new-comer was four and a half inches taller than the medium, had beautiful brown hair, a long tress of which was traced up to the scalp and then severed (Miss Cook was a brunette), and finally that the pulse rate of the two women was entirely different. The whole course of Crookes's life proved that he was neither liar nor lunatic, and so a reasonable man could only believe that this prodigy corroborated by forty photographs was true, but totally unrelated to any other facts of the universe.

But now the matter appears otherwise. Thanks to the recent researchers, we are in a position to enter that darkened room and to reconstruct what is happening to Florrie Cook. She lies with an occasional animal moan upon the sofa. From her there drains the vital ectoplasm, forming a cloud of viscous substance, a pattern, and finally a form. The form disengages, the cord breaks, and Katie King, infusing her spirit into this reconstruction of what was probably a simulacrum of her earthly body, walks forth to spend her strange brief hour upon earth, conversing with Professor Crookes, playing with his children, telling them stories of older days, and finally, with the words, "My mission is finished," leaving them for ever. Her mission was to prove the survival of the spirit to an incredulous generation, and it would indeed have been accomplished had it depended upon the bravery of her witness, and not upon the dense stupidity, prejudice and materialism of the scientific, religious, and journalistic world in which he lived. Now after many days we are slowly understanding the message.

So much for the Crookes episode, and the light which has now been thrown upon it. But there is another famous series of investigations which are also confirmed and illuminated by this new knowledge. These are the very remarkable experiments made by Dr. Crawford, of Belfast, upon the medium Miss Goligher, and described in two successive books, *The Reality of Psychic Phenomena* and *Experiments in Psychic Science*. Miss Goligher, as her portrait indicates, is a young lady of character and education, sprung from a decent Belfast family—a fact which has not prevented our opponents, in their desperate plight for an explanation, from endeavouring without a shred of evidence to depict her as a systematic fraud. It is a deplorable thing that people with this rare power, who submit themselves unpaid for the research of scientific men, should be assailed in this fashion, for it frightens others away, and makes the whole investigation more difficult.

The main lesson, as it seems to me, to be drawn from the Crawford experiments is that the ectoplasm is a substance which can be used for many purposes by the force which lies behind it. In the former cases it was used to build up moulds of the human figure. In the Belfast experiments this same ectoplasm was used for the making of rods or columns of power, which protruded from the body of the unconscious girl, and produced results such as raps, or the movement of objects, at a distance from her. Such a rod of power might be applied, with a sucker attachment, under a table and lift it up, causing the weight of the table to be added to that of the medium, exactly as if she had produced the effect by a steel bar working as a cantilever and attached to her body. Or it might be placed above the table and hold it down, a loss of weight of thirty, forty, or even fifty pounds being registered upon the weighing chair on which Miss Goligher sat. The medium became a mere residuum, with a third and more of her own substance outside herself, the difference showing itself rather in a refining of the whole body than in a visible loss of substance. One can well believe that under such abnormal circumstances any rough disturbance of the conditions which caused the external third to fly back with unnatural speed to the body would cause physical suffering. I have known a medium have a broad weal from breast to armpit through the sudden elastic recoil of the ectoplasm. Is it a wonder, then, that Spiritualists object to the type of researcher who suddenly flashes a powerful electric torch in the middle of a séance? When this matter is more clearly understood our descendants will, I think, be appalled as well as amused by some of the incidents which have been the outcome of our ignorance.

Dr. Crawford's experiments have been an explanation and a justification of the ordinary phenomena of the dark séance. No philosophical unprejudiced mind could have failed to see that results which are always of the same type, whether the conditions be produced in Iceland or in Java, must have fixed laws underlying them. Our critics have continually bemused themselves by considering individual cases and failing to take a broad view of the cumulative evidence. Dr. Crawford makes every detail plain. He has even, by staining with moist carmine a cloth in front of the medium, got crimson marks at a distance showing that the column of force as it pushed forward was solid enough to carry some of the staining agent with it. This is a particularly fine and convincing experiment.

This is but a very brief indication of the general line taken by this remarkable research. Once again a sceptic may say, "But this is physical power of some unknown type and not an intelligence apart from the sitters." A fuller knowledge, however, shows that at every stage there was a controlling intelligence, advising, directing, and showing its wishes by a code of signals. Whose intelligence was it? "I am quite satisfied in my own mind that the operators are discarnate human beings," says Dr. Crawford in his very latest work, with all the results before him. I do not see how anyone else is in a position to go behind his own interpretation of the facts which he has himself made clear. He appears to have begun his investigation in the agnostic attitude, which is the ideal starting-point for the truly scientific mind, but he had the courage and adaptability which made him gain positive results instead of that endless round of experiments leading to no conclusion which is typical of so many psychical researchers.

Such, then, is the story of Mme. Bisson, of Dr. Schrenck-Notzing, of Dr. Geley, of Professor Crookes, and of Dr. Crawford. Can it be laughed away? Is it not time, after seventy years of every-varying proof, that such an attitude be abandoned? But when it is abandoned, and when the conclusions have been accepted, what an eternity of ridicule is waiting for those solemn Panjandrums of Science who have for so long held up their warning hands lest the public should believe the truth!

The story of the Italian Cardinals and Galileo will seem reasonable when compared with the attitude of Victorian science to this invasion of the beyond. Of the theologians I say nothing, for that is another aspect of the matter, and they have only lived up to their own record; but material science, which made mock of mesmerism until for very shame it had to change its name to hypnotism before acknowledging it, has a sad reckoning before it in the case of Spiritualism. The fear is lest the reaction go too far, and in contemplating its colossal blunder we may forget or underrate the thousand additions which it has made to the comfort of the human race.

Be this as it may, who can read the facts here quoted and doubt that in those mists and shadows which hang round this uncharted coast we have at least one solid, clear-cut cape which juts out into the sunshine? Behind, however, lies a hinterland of mystery which successive generations of pioneers will be called upon to explore.

Since this essay was written fresh demonstrations and photographs of ectoplasm have been taken from Mrs. Crandon (Margery) in Boston, from the medium of Dr. Hamilton in Winnipeg, and from Mrs. Henderson of London. If any person can examine all these photographs, taken from such varied subjects, can observe their similarity, and can then doubt that a new field for study has opened up for Science, such a person seems to me to be incapable of receiving a new idea or of forming a sane judgment.

XII

A REMARKABLE MAN

ON THE EARLY MORNING of April 9, 1855, the steam packet *Africa*, from Boston, was drawing into Liverpool Docks. Captain Harrison, his responsibility lifted from him, was standing on the bridge, the pilot beside him, while below the passengers had assembled, some bustling about with their smaller articles of luggage, while others lined the decks and peered curiously at the shores of Old England. Most of them showed natural exultation at the successful end of their voyage, but among them was one who seemed to have no pleasant prospects in view. Indeed, his appearance showed that his most probable destiny would make him independent of any earthly career. This was a youth some two and twenty years of age, tall, slim, with a marked elegance of bearing and a fastidious neatness of dress, but with a worn, hectic look upon his very expressive face, which told of the ravages of some wasting disease. Blue-eyed, and with hair of a light auburn tint, he was of the type which is peculiarly open to the attack of tubercle, and the extreme emaciation of his frame showed how little power remained with him by which he might resist it. An acute physician watching him closely would probably have given him six months of life in our humid island. Yet this young man was destined, as many of us think, to be the instrument in making a greater change in English thought than any traveller for centuries—a change only now slowly developing and destined, as I think, to revolutionize for ever our views on the most

163

vital of all subjects. For this was Daniel Dunglas Home, a youth of Scottish birth and extraction, sprung, it is said, from the noble Border family of that name, and the possessor of strange personal powers which make him, with the possible exception of Swedenborg, the most remarkable individual of whom we have any record since the age of the Apostles, some of whose gifts he appeared to inherit. A deep melancholy lay upon his sensitive features as he viewed the land which contained no one whom he could call friend. Tears welled from his eyes, for he was a man of swift emotions and feminine susceptibilities. Then, with a sudden resolution, he disengaged himself from the crowd, rushed down to the cabin, and fell upon his knees in prayer. He has recorded how a spring of hope and comfort bubbled up in his heart, so that no more joyous man set his foot that day upon the Mersey quay, or one more ready to meet the fate which lay before him.

But how strange a fate, and what a singular equipment with which to face this new world of strangers! He had hardly a relation in the world. His left lung was partly gone. His income was modest, though sufficient. He had no trade or profession, his education having been interrupted by his illness. In character he was shy, gentle, sentimental, artistic, affectionate, and deeply religious. He had a strong tendency both to art and the drama, so that his powers of sculpture were considerable and as a reciter he proved in later life that he had few living equals. But on top of all this, and of an unflinching honesty which was so uncompromising that he often offended his own allies, there was one gift so remarkable that it threw everything else into significance. This lay in certain powers, quite independent of his own volition, coming and going with disconcerting suddenness, but proving to all who would examine the proof that there was something in this man's atmosphere which enabled forces outside himself and outside our ordinary apprehension to manifest themselves upon this plane of matter. In other words, he was a medium—the greatest on the physical side that the modern world has ever seen.

A lesser man might have used his extraordinary powers to found some special sect of which he would have been the undisputed high priest, or to surround himself with a glamour of power and mystery. Certainly most people in his position would have been tempted to use them for the making of money. As to this latter point, let it be said at once that never in the course of the thirty years of his strange ministry did he touch one shilling as payment for his gifts. It is on sure record that as much as two thousand pounds was offered to him by the Union Circle in Paris in the year 1857 for a single séance, and that he, a poor man and an invalid, utterly refused. "I have been sent on a mission," he said; "that mission is to demonstrate immortality. I have never taken money for it, and I never will." There were certain presents from Royalty which cannot be refused without boorishness—rings, scarf pins, and the like, tokens of friendship rather than recompense, for before his premature death there were few monarchs in Europe with whom this shy youth from the Liverpool landing-stage was not upon terms of affectionate intimacy. Napoleon the Third provided for his only sister; the Emperor of Russia sponsored his marriage. What novelist would dare to invent such a career?

But there are more subtle temptations than those of wealth. Home's uncompromising honesty was the best safeguard against those. Never for a moment did he lose his humility and his sense of proportion. "I have these powers," he would say: "I shall be happy up to the limit of my strength to demonstrate them to you if you approach me as one gentleman should approach another. I shall be glad if you can throw any further light upon them. I will lend myself to any reasonable experiment. I have no control over them—they use me but I do not use them. They desert me for months and then come back in redoubled force. I am a passive instrument—no more." Such was his unvarying attitude. He was always the easy, amiable man of the world with nothing either of the mantle of the prophet or of the skull-cap of the magician. Like most truly great men, there was no touch of pose in his nature. An index of his fine feeling is that when confirmation was needed for his results he would never quote any names unless he was perfectly certain that the owners would not suffer in any way through being associated with an unpopular cult. Sometimes, even after they had freely given leave, he still withheld the names, lest he should unwittingly injure a friend. When he published his first series of *Incidents in My Life* the *Saturday Review* waxed very sarcastic over the anonymous evidence of Countess O——, Count B——, Count de K——, Princess de B——, and Mrs. S——, who were quoted as having witnessed manifestations. In his second volume Home, having assured himself of the concurrence of his friends, filled the blanks with the names of the Countess Orsini, Count de Beaumont, Count de Komar, Princess de Beaurean, and the well-known American hostess, Mrs. Henry Senior. His Royal friends he never quoted at all, and yet it is notorious that the Emperor Napoleon III, the Empress Eugénie, the Czar, the Emperor William I of Germany, and the Kings of Bavaria and Wurtemberg were all equally convinced by his extraordinary powers. Never once was Home convicted of any deception either in word or in deed.

In these days, when the facts of psychic phenomena are familiar to all save those who are wilfully ignorant, we can hardly realize the moral courage which was needed by Home in putting forward his powers and upholding them in public. To the average educated Briton in the material Victorian era, a man who claimed to be able to produce results which upset Newton's law of gravity, and which showed invisible mind acting upon visible matter, was *prima facie* a scoundrel and an imposter. The view of Spiritualism pronounced by Vice-Chancellor Gifford at the conclusion of the Home-Lyon trial was that of the class to which he belonged. He knew nothing of the matter, but took it for granted that anything with such claims must be false. No doubt similar things were reported in far-off lands and ancient books, but that they could occur in prosaic, steady old England, the England of bank rates and free imports, was too absurd for serious thought. It has been recorded that at this trial Lord Gifford turned to Home's counsel and said, "Do I understand you to state that your client claims that he has been levitated into the air?" The counsel assented, on which the judge turned to the jury and made such a movement as the high-priest may have made in ancient days when he rent his garments as a protest against blasphemy. In 1867 there were few of the jury who were sufficiently educated to check the judge's remarks, and it is just in that particular that we have made some progress in the fifty years between. Slow work; but Christianity took more than three hundred years to come into its own.

Take this question of levitation as a test of Home's powers. It is claimed that more than a hundred times in good light, before reputable witnesses, he floated in the air. Consider the evidence. In 1857, in a château near Bordeaux, he was lifted to the ceiling of a lofty room in the presence of Mme. Ducos, widow of the Minister of Marine, and of the Count and Countess de Beaumont. In 1860 Robert Bell wrote an article, "Stranger than Fiction," in the *Cornhill*. "He rose from his chair," says Bell, "four or five feet from the ground. . . . We saw his figure pass from one side of the window to the other, feet foremost, lying horizontally in the air." Dr. Gully, of Malvern, a well-known medical man, and Robert Chambers, the author and publisher, were the other witnesses. Is it to be supposed that these men were lying confederates, or that they could not tell if a man were floating in the air or pretending to do so? In the same year Home was raised at Mrs. Milner Gibson's house in the presence of Lord and Lady Clarence Paget—the former passing his hands underneath him to assure himself of the fact. A few months later, Mr. Wason, a Liverpool solicitor, with seven others saw the same phenomenon. "Mr. Home," he says, "crossed the table over the heads of the persons sitting around it." He added: "I reached his hand seven feet from the floor, and moved along five or six paces as he floated above me in the air." In 1861 Mrs. Parkes, of Cornwall Terrace, Regent's Park, tells how she was present with Bulwer Lytton and Mr. Hall when Home, in her own drawing-room, was raised till his hand was on the top of the door, and then floated horizontally forwards. In 1866 Mr. and Mrs. Hall, Lady Dunsany and Mrs. Senior, in Mr. Hall's house, saw Home, his face transfigured and shining, twice rise to the ceiling, leaving a cross marked in pencil upon the second occasion, so as to assure the witnesses that they were not victims of imagination. In 1868 Lord Adare, Lord Lindsay, Captain Wynne, and Mr. Smith Barry saw Home levitate upon many occasions. A very minute account has been left by the first three witnesses of the occurrence of December 16 of this year, when, at Ashley House, Home, in a state of trance, floated out of the bedroom and into the sitting-room window, passing seventy feet above the street. After his arrival in the sitting-room he went back into the bedroom with Lord Adare, and upon the latter remarking that he could not understand how Home could have floated through the window, which was only partially raised, "he told me to stand a little distance off. He then went through the open space head first quite rapidly, his body being nearly horizontal and apparently rigid. He came in again feet foremost." Such was the account given by Lords Adare and Lindsay. Upon its publication, Dr. Carpenter, who earned an unenviable reputation by a perverse opposition to every fact which bore upon this question, wrote exultantly to point out that there had been a third witness who had not been heard from, assuming, without the least justification, that Captain Wynne's evidence would be contradictory. He went the length of saying, "A single honest sceptic declares that Mr. Home was sitting in his chair all the time," a statement which can only be described as false. Captain Wynne at once wrote corroborating the others, and adding, "If you are not to believe the corroborative evidence of *three* unimpeached witnesses, there would be an end to all justice and courts of law." So many are the other instances of Home's levitations that a long article might easily be written upon this single phase of his mediumship. Professor Crookes was again and again a witness to the phenomenon, and refers to fifty instances which had come within his knowledge. But is there any fair-minded person, who has read the little that I have recorded above, who will not say with Professor Challis, "Either the facts must be admitted or the possibility of certifying facts by human testimony must be given up"?

But now a word of explanation. "Are we then back in the age of miracles?" cries the reader. There is no miracle—nothing on this plane is supernatural. What we see now and what we have read of in ages past are but the operation of law which has not yet been studied and defined. Already we realize something of its possibilities and of its limitations, which are as exact in their way as those of any purely physical power. We must hold the balance between those who would believe nothing and those who would believe too much. Gradually the mists will clear and we will chart the shadowy coast. When the needle first sprang up at the magnet it was not an infraction of the laws of gravity. It was that there had been the local intervention of another, stronger force. Such is the case, also, when psychic powers act upon the plane of matter. Had Home's faith in this power faltered, or had his circle been unduly disturbed, he would have fallen. When Peter lost faith he sank into the waves. Across the centuries the same cause still produced the same effect. Spiritual power is ever with us if we do not avert our faces, and nothing has been vouchsafed to Judea which is withheld from England.

It is in this respect, as a confirmation of the power of the unseen, and as a final answer to materialism as we now understand it, that Home's public career is of such supreme importance. He was an affirmative witness of the truth of those so-called "miracles," which have been the stumbling-block for so many earnest minds, and are now destined to be the strong, solid proof of the accuracy of the original narrative. Millions of doubting souls in the agony of spiritual conflict had cried out for definite proof that all was not empty space around us, that there were powers beyond our grasp, that the ego was not a mere secretion of nervous tissue, and that the dead did really carry on this personal, unbroken, existence. All this was proved by this greatest of modern missionaries to anyone who could observe and reason. It is easy to poke superficial fun at rising tables and quivering walls, but they were the nearest and most natural objects which could record in material terms that power which was beyond our human ken. A mind which would be unmoved by an inspired sentence was struck into humility and into new paths of research in the presence of even the most homely of these inexplicable phenomena. It is easy to call them puerile, but they effected the purpose for which they were sent by shaking to its foundations the complaisance of those material men of science who were brought into actual contact with them. They are to be regarded not as ends in themselves, but as the elementary means by which the mind should be diverted into new channels of thought. And those channels of thought led straight to the recognition of the survival of the spirit. "You have conveyed incalculable joy and comfort to the hearts of many people," said Bishop Clark of Rhode Island. "You have made dwelling-places light that were dark before." "Mademoiselle," said Home to the lady who was to be his wife, "I have a mission entrusted to me; it is a great and a holy one." The famous Dr. Elliotson, immortalized by Thackeray under the name of Dr. Goodenough, was one of the leaders of British materialism. He met Home, saw his powers, and was able soon to say that he had lived all his life in darkness and had thought there was nothing in existence but the material; but he now had a firm hope which he trusted he would hold while on earth. Innumerable instances could be quoted of the spiritual value of his work but it has never been better summed up than in a paragraph from Mrs. Webster, of Florence, who saw much of his ministry. "He is the most marvellous missionary of modern times, in the greatest of all causes, and the good that he has done cannot be reckoned. Where Mr. Home passes he bestows around him the greatest of all blessings— the certainty of a future life." Now that the details of his career can be read it is to the whole wide world that he brings this most vital of all messages.

It is curious to see how his message affected those of his own generation. Reading the account of his life written by his widow—a most convincing document, since she, of all living mortals, must have known the real man—it would appear that his most utterly whole-hearted support and appreciation came from those aristocrats of France and Russia with whom he was brought into contact. The warm glow of personal admiration and even reverence in their letters is such as can hardly be matched in any biography. In England he had a close circle of ardent supporters, a few of the upper classes, with the Halls, the Howitts, Robert Chambers, Mrs. Milner Gibson, Professor Crookes, and others. But there was a sad lack of courage among those who admitted the facts in private and stood aloof in public. Lord Brougham and Bulwer Lytton were of the type of Nicodemus, the novelist being the worst offender. The "Intelligentsia" on the whole came badly out of the matter, and many an honoured name suffers in the story. Faraday and Tyndall were fantastically unscientific in their methods of prejudging a question first, and offering to examine it afterwards on the condition that their prejudgment was accepted. Sir David Brewster said some honest things, and then, in a panic, denied that he had said them, forgetting that the evidence was on actual record. Browning wrote a long poem—if such doggerel can be called poetry—to describe an exposure which had never taken place. Carpenter earned an unenviable notoriety as an unscrupulous opponent, while proclaiming some strange spiritualistic thesis of his own. The secretaries of the Royal Society refused to take a cab drive in order to see Crookes' demonstration of the physical phenomena, while they pronounced roundly against them. Lord Gifford inveighed from the Bench against a subject the first elements of which he did not understand. As to the clergy, such an order might not have existed during the thirty years that this, the most marvellous spiritual outpouring of many centuries, was before the public. I cannot recall the name of one British clergyman who showed any intelligent interest, and when in 1872 a full account of the St. Petersburg séances began to appear in *The Times*, it was cut short, according to Mr. H. T. Humphreys, "on account of strong remonstrances to Mr. Delane, the editor, by certain of the higher clergy of the Church of England." Such was the contribution of our official spiritual guides. Dr. Elliotson, the Rationalist, was far more alive than they. The rather bitter comment of Mrs. Home is: "This verdict of his own generation was that of the blind and deaf upon the man who could hear and see."

Home's charity was among his more beautiful characteristics. Like all charity, it was secret, and only comes out indirectly and by chance. One of his numerous traducers declared that he had allowed a bill for fifty pounds to be sent in to his friend, Mr. Rhymer. In self-defence it came out that it was not a bill, but a cheque most generously sent by Home to help this friend in a crisis. Considering his constant poverty, fifty pounds probably represented a good part of his bank balance. His widow dwells with pardonable pride upon the many evidences found in his letters after his death. "Now it is an unknown artist for whose brush Home's generous efforts had found employment; now a distressed worker writes of his sick wife's life saved by comforts that Home provided; now a mother thanks him for a start in life for her son. How much time and thought he devoted to helping others when the circumstances of his own life would have led most men to think only of their own needs and cares." "Send me a word from the heart that has known so often how to cheer a friend!" cries one of his *protégés*. "Shall I ever prove worthy of all the good you have done me?" says another letter. We find him roaming the battlefields round Paris, often under fire, with his pockets full of cigars for the wounded. A German officer writes affectionately to remind him how he saved him from bleeding to death, and carried him on his own weak back out of the place of danger. Truly Mrs. Browning was a better judge of character than her spouse, and Sir Galahad a better name than Sludge.

There are few of the varied gifts which we call "mediumistic," and St. Paul "of the spirit," which Home did not possess—indeed, the characteristic of his psychic power was its unusual versatility. We speak usually of a direct voice medium, of a trance speaker, of a clairvoyant, or of a physical medium, but Home was all four. To take St. Paul's gifts in their order he had "the word of wisdom and the word of knowledge" when in his trance utterances he described the life beyond. "The gift of healing" was with him, and the account of his curing young De Cardonne of total deafness or of Mme. de Lakine of paralysis is historical. "The operation of great works" was shown in his phenomena when the very building would shake from an unknown power. "Discerning of spirits," was continually with him. There is no note, however, of prophecy or of the gift of tongues. So far as can be traced, he had little experience of the powers of other mediums, and was not immune from that psychic jealousy which is a common trait of these sensitives. Mrs. Jencken, formerly Miss Kate Fox, was the only other medium with whom he was upon terms of friendship. He bitterly resented any form of deception, and carried this excellent trait rather too far by looking with eyes of suspicion upon all forms of manifestation which did not exactly correspond with his own. This opinion, expressed in an uncompromising manner in his last book, *Lights and Shadows of Spiritualism,* gave natural offence to other mediums, who claimed to be as honest as himself. A wider acquaintance with phenomena would have made him more charitable. Thus he protested strongly against any séance being held in the dark, but this is certainly a counsel of perfection, for experiments upon the ectoplasm, which is the physical basis of all materializations, show that it is fatally affected by light unless it is tinted red. Home had no large experience of complete materializations, such as those obtained in those days by Miss Florrie Cook or Mme. d'Esperance or in our own time by Mme. Bisson's medium, and therefore he could dispense with complete darkness in his own ministry. Thus his opinion was unjust to others. Again, Home declared roundly that matter could not pass through matter, because his own phenomena did not take that form, and yet the evidence that matter can in certain cases be passed through matter seems to be overwhelming. Even birds of rare varieties have been brought into séance rooms under circumstances which seem to preclude fraud, and the experiments of passing wood through wood as shown before Zöllner and the other Leipzig professors were quite final, as set forth in the famous physicist's account, in *Transcendental Physics* of his experiences with Salde. Thus it may count as a small flaw in Home's character that he decried and doubted the powers which he did not himself happen to possess.

Some also might count it as a failing that he carried his message rather to the leaders of society and of life than to the vast toiling masses. It is probable that Home had, in fact, the weakness as well as the graces of the artistic nature, and that he was most at ease and happiest in an atmosphere of elegance and refinement, with a personal repulsion from all that was sordid and ill-favoured. If there were no other reason, the precarious state of his health unfitted him for any sterner mission, and he was driven by repeated haemorrhages to seek the pleasant and refined life of Italy, Switzerland, and the Riviera. But for the prosecution of his mission, as apart from personal self-sacrifice, there can be no doubt that his message carried to the laboratory of a Crookes or to the court of a Napoleon was more useful than if it were laid before the crowd. The assent of science and of character was needed before the public could gain assurance that such things were true. If it was not fully gained, the fault lies assuredly with the hide bound men of science and thinkers of the day, and by no means with Home, who played his part of actual demonstration to perfection, leaving it to other and less gifted men to analyse and to make public that which he had shown them. He did not profess to be a man of science, but he was the raw material of science, willing and anxious that others should learn from him all that he could convey to the world, so that science should itself testify to religion, while religion should be buttressed upon science. When Home's message has been fully learned, an unbelieving man will not stand convicted of impiety, but of ignorance.

There was something pathetic in Home's efforts to find some creed in which he could satisfy his own gregarious instinct—for he had no claims to be a strong-minded individualist—and at the same time find a niche into which he could fit his own precious packet of assured truth. His pilgrimage vindicates the assertion of some Spiritualists that a man may belong to any creed and carry with him the spiritual knowledge, but it also bears out those who reply that perfect harmony with that spiritual knowledge can only be found, as matters now stand, in a special Spiritualist community. Alas, that it should be so! For it is too big a thing to sink into a sect, however great that sect might become. Home began in his youth as a Wesleyan, but soon left them for the more liberal atmosphere of Congregationalism. In Italy the artistic atmosphere of the Roman Catholic Church, and possibly its record of so many phenomena, akin to his own, caused him to become a convert with an intention of joining a monastic order—an intention which his common sense caused him to abandon. The change of religion was at a period when his psychic powers had deserted him for a year, and his confessor assured him that as they were of evil origin they would certainly never be heard of again now that he was a son of the true Church. None the less, on the very day that the year expired they came back in renewed strength. From that time Home seemed to have been only nominally a Catholic if at all, and after his second marriage—both his marriages were to Russian ladies—he was strongly drawn towards the Greek Church, and it was under their ritual that he was at last laid to rest at St. Germain in 1886. "To another of spirits" (I Cor. xii. 10) is the short inscription upon that grave, of which the world has not yet heard the last.

If proof were needed of the blamelessness of Home's life, it could not be better shown than by the fact that his numerous enemies, spying ever for some opening to attack, could get nothing in his whole career upon which to comment save the wholly innocent affair which is known as the Home-Lyon case. Any impartial judge, reading the depositions in this case—they are to be found verbatim in the second series of *Incidents from My Life*—would agree that it is not blame but commiseration which was owing to Home. One could desire no higher proof of the nobility of his character than his dealings with this unpleasant, freakish woman, who first insisted upon settling a large sum of money upon him, and then, her whim having changed and her expectations of an immediate introduction into high society being disappointed, stuck at nothing in order to get it back again.

Had she merely asked for it back, there is little doubt that Home's delicate feelings would have led him to return it, even though he had been put to much trouble and expense over the matter, which had entailed a change of his name to Home-Lyon, to meet the woman's desire that he should be her adopted son. Her request, however, was so framed that he could not honourably agree to it, as it would have implied an admission that he had done wrong in accepting the gift. If one consults the original letters—which few of those who comment upon the case seem to have done—you find that Home, S. C. Hall as his representative, and Mr. Wilkinson as his solicitor, implored the woman to moderate the unreasonable benevolence which was to change so rapidly into even more unreasonable malevolence. She was absolutely determined that Home should have the money and be her heir. A less mercenary man never lived, and he begged her again and again to think of her relatives, to which she answered that the money was her own to do what she pleased with, and that no relatives were dependent upon it. From the time that he accepted the new situation he acted and wrote as a dutiful son, and it is not uncharitable to suppose that this entirely filial attitude may not have been that which this elderly lady had planned out in her scheming brain. At any rate, she soon tired of her fad and reclaimed her money upon the excuse—a monstrous one to anyone who will read the letters and consider the dates—that spirit messages received through Home had caused her to take the action she had done. The case was tried in the Court of Chancery, and the judge alluded to Mrs. Lyon's "innumerable misstatements on many important particulars—misstatements upon oath so perversely untrue that they have embarrassed the Court to a great degree and quite discredited the plaintiff's testimony." In spite of this caustic comment, and in spite also of elementary justice, the verdict was against Home on the general ground that British law put the burden of disproof upon the defendant in such a case, and complete disproof is impossible when assertion is met by counterassertion. Even Home's worst enemies were forced to admit that the fact that he had retained the money in England and had not lodged it where it would have been beyond recovery, proved his honest intentions in this the most unfortunate episode of his life.

Such, within the compass of a short sketch, was the strange fate of the young man whom we saw land upon the Liverpool pier. He was at that time twenty-two. He died in his fifty-third year. In those thirty years he threw out seed with either hand. Much fell among stones; much was lost on the wayside; but much found a true resting-place, and has put forth a harvest the end of which no living man can see.

XIII

THE RIFT IN THE VEIL

WHETHER THE READER belongs to that majority who are incredulous upon the subject, or to that increasing minority who accept the evidence, he can hardly fail to be interested in the circumstances in which the whole strange psychic movement arose. The student is aware that there was a long preparatory stage which began with Swedenborg and Mesmer, and ended with Andrew Jackson Davis, called the Poughkeepsie seer, who at an early age, without education, wrote or dictated one of the deepest, most comprehensive explanations of the universe, ever framed. Passing these we will begin the narrative with the happenings of Hydesville, and give some account of these less-known developments which followed the new movement, sometimes to its great glory and sometimes to its temporary degradation.

The hamlet of Hydesville, near Rochester, in the State of New York, consisted of a cluster of wooden houses of a very humble type. In one of these, a residence which would hardly pass the requirement of a British district council surveyor, there began this development which will, in my opinion, prove to be far the most important thing which America has given to the common weal of the world. It was inhabited by a decent farmer family of the name of Fox—a name which, by a curious coincidence, has been already registered in religious history as that of the evangel of the Quakers. Beside the father and mother, who were Methodists in religion, there were two children resident in the house at the time when the manifestations reached such a point of intensity that they attracted general attention. These children were the daughters, Margaret, aged fifteen, and Kate, aged twelve.

About the beginning of 1848 many loud noises like sudden blows had been heard both by day and by night in the house, accompanied by a vibration of the furniture. Rats, mice and the hammering of a neighbouring cobbler were all put forward as explanations and each proved equally inadequate. As the spring advanced these sounds became more insistent and more varied in character, and occasionally were accompanied by actual motions of the furniture. It was soon observed that daylight was inimical to the phenomena, and the idea of trickery was thereby suggested, but careful watch by Mr. Fox failed to detect anything of the kind. Finally, on March 31st, there was a very loud and continued outbreak of inexplicable sounds. It was upon this evening that one of the great points in the history of psychic evolution was reached, for it was then that young Kate Fox, having lost all sense of fear in the presence of that which use had made familiar, challenged the unseen power to repeat the snaps of her fingers. This challenge, though given in flippant words, was instantly accepted. Each snap was answered by a knock. However humble the operator at either end, the spiritual telegraph was at last working, and it was left to the patience and moral earnestness of the human race to determine how high might be the uses to which it was put in the future. Unexplained forces were many in the world, but here was a force claiming to have independent intelligence at the back of it. That was the supreme sign of a new departure. "Fancy a new spiritual departure in a frame-house in an American hamlet!" Yes, and fancy a previous one in a camel-driver's tent in Arabia, and before that the greatest of all in a carpenter's shop in Judea! *Exaltavit humiles!*

Mrs. Fox was amazed at this development, and at the further discovery that the force could apparently see as well as hear, for when Kate snapped her fingers without sound the rap still responded. The mother asked a series of questions, the answers to which, given in numerals, showed a greater knowledge of her own affairs than she herself possessed, for the raps insisted that she had had seven children, whereas she protested that she had six, until one who had died early came back to her mind. A neighbour, Mrs. Redfield, was called in, and her amusement was changed to wonder, and finally to awe, as she also listened to the correct answers to intimate questions.

The neighbours came flocking in as some rumours of these wonders got about, and the two children were carried off by one of them, while Mrs. Fox went to spend the night at Mrs. Redfield's. In their absence the phenomena went on exactly the same as before, which disposes once for all of those theories of cracking toes and dislocating knees which have been so frequently put forward by people unaware of the true facts. The happenings of the night were at once recorded and were printed in pamphlet form within three weeks of the event, so that it would be difficult to get more prompt and direct testimony, which was subscribed to by a number of disinterested witnesses.

Having formed a sort of informal committee of investigation, the crowd, in shrewd Yankee fashion, spent a large part of the night of March 31st in playing question and answer with the unseen intelligence. According to its own account he was a spirit, he had been injured in that house, he rapped out the name of a former occupant who had injured him, he was thirty-one years old at the time of death, which was five years before, he had been murdered for money, he had been buried in the cellar ten feet deep. On descending to the cellar dull, heavy thumps, coming apparently from under the earth, broke out when the investigator stood at the centre. There was no sound at other times. That, then, was the place of burial! It was a neighbour named Duesler who, first of all modern men, called over the alphabet and got answers by raps on the letters. In this way the name of the dead man was obtained—Charles B. Rosma. The idea of connected messages was not developed until four months later, when Isaac Post, a Quaker of Rochester, was the first pioneer. Such, in very brief outline, were the events of March 31st, which were continued and confirmed upon the succeeding night, when not less than a couple of hundred people had assembled round the house. Upon April 2nd, it was observed that the raps came in the day as well as at night.

Excavations were begun in the cellar, but the spring thaw and a swollen river had flooded the land, and water was struck a foot or so below the surface. When the summer came, a hole was dug by David Fox, the young son, who had come from a distant farm after the disturbances broke out. He was aided by Henry Bush, Lyman Granger of Rochester, and others. His account of what occurred was published in Capron's *Modern Spiritualism*, 1855, and was confirmed personally in conversation with the Hon. Dale Owen, so that the evidence is very clear and direct. They passed a plank five feet down, and below it came on some crockery, charcoal, and quicklime, under which was some human hair, several bones, and part of a human skull. Clearer evidence of murder and its concealment could hardly be asked for. These were corroborative details, for a young girl, Lucretia Pulver, came forward with an account of how a pedlar had called there while she was acting as "help" to Mr. and Mrs. B——. He had remained for the night, while she, the girl, had been sent away, and was kept away three days. The pedlar had promised to call at her father's house, but he never came. On her return she had heard for the first time the rappings and noises in the house. She observed that the centre of the cellar was soft, which was explained by Mrs. B—— as being due to ratholes. Afterwards, Mr. B—— carried down some earth and was at work for some time. Shortly afterwards the B——s left the house and the neighbourhood, but their successors, the Weekmans, were conscious of the same noises which finally culminated under the Fox tenancy.

As might be expected, B——, who was a blacksmith by trade, vigorously denied this accusation and produced many certificates as a proof that he was a man of good character. The spiritual story was also weakened by the fact that the man Rosma could not be traced in Orange County, New York, whence he professed to have come, and a search for five alleged children was equally fruitless. We know now how difficult it is to get a name through correctly, and I think it very likely that "Ross" may have been the real surname. His non-recognition is less remarkable as he was by profession a wanderer. It must be admitted that the case against B—— needed further corroboration before it could be called substantial. Two great undoubted results did emerge, however, which have never been shaken, that the origin of the raps could by no means be explained, and that they did convey the unknown fact that a human body had been buried in the cellar. This is the vital core of the whole matter, for it touched that which is of eternal interest to all of us, while the question of individual guilt is temporary and incidental.

The danger of blindly following alleged spirit guidance was clearly shown some months later in the neighbouring town of Rochester, where a man disappeared under suspicious circumstances. An enthusiastic Spiritualist had messages by raps which announced a murder. The canal was dragged, and the wife of the missing man was actually ordered to enter the canal, which nearly cost her her life. Some months later the absentee returned, having fled to Canada to avoid a writ for debt. This, as may well be imagined, was a blow to the young cult. The public did not then understand what even now is so little understood, that death causes no change in the human spirit, that mischievous and humorous entities abound, and that the inquirer must use his own instincts and his own common sense at every turn. "Try the spirits that ye may know them." In the same year, in the same district, the truth of this new philosophy upon the one side, and its limitations and dangers on the other, were most clearly set forth. These dangers are with us still. The silly man, the arrogant inflated man, the cock-sure man, is always a safe butt. Every observer has had some trick played upon him. I have myself had my faith sorely shaken by deception until some compensating proof has come along to assure me that it was only a lesson which I had received, and that it was no more fiendish or even remarkable that disembodied intelligences should be hoaxers, than that the same intelligence inside a human body should find amusement in the same foolish way.

The first effect of the new dispensation was to bring utter misery and ruin to the Fox family. Within their house there were constant disturbances from the insistent manifestations, while from without they were plagued by sightseers and wonder-mongers, many of whom looked upon the unfortunate people as being concerned in something diabolical. Kate was sent away to Rochester to join her married sister, Mrs. Fish, but her absence appears to have had no effect upon the sounds which continued to disturb the family, who at last abandoned Hydesville altogether, hoping that the manifestations would remain behind. It speedily became evident, however, that the unseen powers were no longer attached to the place, but that they specially associated themselves with the two girls, for they were as insistent in the town as in the hamlet. In vain the family prayed with their Methodist friends that relief should come. In vain also were the exorcisms of the ministers of various creeds. Beyond joining with loud raps in the "Amens," the unseen presences took no notice of these religious exercises.

The whole course of the movement had now widened and taken a more important turn. It was no longer a murdered man calling for justice. The pedlar seemed to have been used as a pioneer, and now that he had found the opening and the method, a myriad of Intelligences were swarming at his back. Isaac Post had instituted the method of spelling by raps, and messages were pouring through. According to these the whole system had been devised by the contrivance of a band of thinkers and inventors upon the spirit plane, foremost among whom was Benjamin Franklin, whose eager mind and electrical knowledge in earth life might well qualify him for such a venture. Whether this claim was true or not, it is a fact that Rosma dropped out of the picture at this stage, and that the intelligent knockings purported to be from the deceased friends of those inquirers who were prepared to take a serious interest in the matter, and to gather in reverent mood to receive the messages. That they still lived and still loved was the constant message from the beyond, accompanied by many material tests, which confirmed the wavering faith of the new adherents of the movement. When asked for their methods of working and the laws which governed them, the answers were from the beginning exactly what they are now—that it was a matter concerned with human and spirit magnetism, that some who were richly endowed with this physical property were mediums, that this endowment was not necessarily allied to morality or intelligence, and that the condition of harmony was especially necessary to secure good results. In eighty years we have learned very little more—and after all these years the primary law of harmony is invariably broken at the so-called test séances, the members of which imagine that they have disproved the philosophy when they obtain no results, whereas they have actually confirmed it.

In one of the early communications the Fox sisters were assured that "these manifestations would go all over the world." This prophecy was soon in a fair way to be fulfilled, for these new powers, and further developments of them which included the discerning and hearing of spirits and the movement of objects without contact, appeared in many circles which were independent of the Fox family. In an incredibly short space of time the movement, with many eccentricities and phases of fanaticism, had swept over the Northern and Eastern States of the Union, always retaining that solid core of actual tangible fact, which might be occasionally simulated by impostors but always reasserted itself to the serious investigator who could shake himself free from preconceived prejudice. Disregarding for the moment these wider developments, let us continue the story of the original circles at Rochester.

The spirit messages had urged upon the small band of pioneers a public demonstration of their powers in an open meeting at Rochester —a proposition which was naturally appalling to two shy country girls and to their friends. So incensed were the discarnate Guides by the opposition of their earthly agents, that they threatened to suspend the whole movement for a generation, and did actually desert them completely for some weeks. At the end of that time communication was restored, and the believers, chastened by this interval of thought, put themselves unreservedly into the hands of the outside forces, promising that they would dare all in the cause. It was no light matter. A few of the clergy, notably a Methodist named the Rev. A. H. Jervis, rallied to their aid, but the majority thundered from their pulpits against them, and the mob eagerly joined in the cowardly sport of heretic-baiting. On November 14, 1849, the Spiritualists held their first meeting at the Corinthian Hall, the largest available in Rochester. The audience, to its credit, listened with attention to the exposition of facts from Mr. Capron of Auburn, the principal speaker. A committee of five representative citizens was then selected to examine into the matter and to report upon the following evening, when the meeting would reassemble. So certain was it that this report would be unfavourable that the *Rochester Democrat* is stated to have had its leading article prepared, with the heading: "Entire Exposure of the Rapping Humbug." The result however, caused the editor to hold his hand. The committee reported that the raps were undoubted facts, though the information was not invariably correct. They added that these raps came on walls and doors some distance from the girls, causing a sensible vibration. "They entirely failed to find any means by which it could be done."

This report was received with disapproval by the audience and a second committee from among the dissentients was formed. This investigation was conducted in the office of a lawyer. Kate, for some reason, was away, and only Mrs. Fish and Margaret present. None the less, the sounds continued as before, though a Dr. Langworthy was introduced to test the possibility of ventriloquism. The final report was that "the sounds were heard, and their thorough investigation had conclusively shown them to be produced neither by machinery nor ventriloquism, though what the agent is they were unable to determine."

Again the audience turned down the report of their own committee, and again a deputation was chosen from among the most extreme opponents, one of whom vowed that if he could not find out the trick he would throw himself over the Falls of the Genessee River. Their examination was thorough to the length of brutality, and a committee of ladies were associated with it. The latter stripped the frightened girls, who wept bitterly under their afflictions. Their dresses were then tied tightly round their ankles, and they were placed upon glass and other insulators. The committee was forced to report "when they were standing on pillows with a handkerchief tied round the bottom of their dresses, tight to the ankles, we all heard the rapping on the wall and floor distinctly." The committee further testified that their questions, some of them mental, had been answered correctly.

So long as the public looked upon the movement as a sort of joke it was prepared to be tolerantly amused, but when these successive reports put the matter in a more serious light, a wave of blackguardism swept over the town, which reached such a pitch that Mr. Willetts, a gallant Quaker, was compelled at the fourth public meeting to declare that "the mob of ruffians who designed to lynch the girls should do so, if they attempted it, over his dead body." There was a disgraceful riot, the young women were smuggled out by a back door, and reason and justice were for the moment clouded over by force and folly. Then, as now, the minds of the average men of the world were so crammed with the things that do not matter that they had no space for the things that do matter. But Fate is never in a hurry and the movement went on. Many accepted the findings of the successive committees as being final, and indeed it is difficult to see how the alleged facts could have been more severely tested. At the same time this strong new fermenting wine began to burst some of the old bottles into which it was poured, to to the excusable disgust of the public.

The many discreet, serious, and religious circles were for a season almost obscured by swollen-headed ranters, who imagined themselves to be in touch with every high entity from the Apostles downwards, some even claiming the direct afflatus of the Holy Ghost and emitting messages which were only saved from being blasphemous by their crudity and absurdity. One community of these fanatics, who called themselves the Apostolic Circle of Mountain Cove, particularly distinguished themselves by their extreme claims and furnished good material for the enemies of the new dispensation. The great body of Spiritualists turned away in disapproval from such exaggerations, but were unable to prevent them. Many well-attested supernormal phenomena came to support the failing spirits of those who were distressed by the excesses of the fanatics. On one occasion, which is particularly convincing and well-reported, two bodies of investigators in separate rooms received the same messages simultaneously from some central force which called itself Benjamin Franklin. This double message was: "There will be great changes in the nineteenth century. Things that now look dark will be made plain. The world will be enlightened." It must be admitted that the prophecy has up to now been only partially fulfilled—and it may at the same time be conceded that, with some startling exceptions, the forecasts of the Spirit people have not been remarkable for accuracy, especially where the element of time is concerned.

The question has often been asked: "What was the purpose of so strange a movement at this particular time, granting that it is all that it claims to be?" Governor Tallmadge, a United States Senator of repute, was one of the early converts to the new cult, and he has left it upon record that he asked this question upon two separate occasions in two different years from different mediums. The answer in each case was almost identical. The first said: "It is to draw mankind together in harmony and to convince sceptics of the immortality of the soul." The second said: "To unite mankind and to convince sceptics of the immortality of the soul." Surely this is no ignoble ambition and does not justify those narrow and bitter attacks from ministers and the less progressive of their flocks from which Spiritualists have up to the present day had to suffer. The first half of the definition is, I think, particularly important, for I believe that one of the ultimate results of his movement will be to unite Christianity upon a common basis so strong and, indeed, self-sufficient that the quibbles which separate the Churches of to-day will be seen in their true proportion and will be swept away or disregarded. One could even hope that such a movement might spread beyond the bounds of Christianity and throw down some of the barriers which stand between great sections of the human race.

Within two years from the crisis at Hydesville, the Fox sisters, still little more than children, were in New York, in the centre of the huge public discussion which raged round the subject. They stayed as guests for a short time in the house of Horace Greeley, the famous editor of the *New York Tribune*, one of the clearest thinkers in America, and whilst there gave constant exhibitions of their strange powers. Greeley had the courage to imperil the fortunes of his great newspaper by publicly stating that the phenomena which he had tested were undoubtedly genuine. "We devoted what time we could spare from our duties, out of three days, to this subject," he wrote:

"It would be the basest cowardice not to say that we are convinced beyond a doubt of the ladies' perfect integrity and good faith. Whatever may be the origin or cause of the rappings, the ladies in whose presence they occur do not make them. We tested this thoroughly and to our entire satisfaction. Their conduct and bearing are as unlike that of deceivers as possible."

So said Horace Greeley, cute Yankee and man of the world, after personal investigation. Against this, what is the worth of the opinion of people who even now talk nonsense about cracking joints and ventriloquism?

What impressed the New Yorkers as much as the actual sounds was the extreme accuracy of the answers and the fact that unspoken questions were replied to as readily as those which were audible. We have records of one particular séance at which there were more famous men assembled than have ever perhaps been present at one demonstration. Among them were Fenimore Cooper, the novelist; Bancroft, the historian; Cullen Bryant and N. P. Willis, poets; Bigelow, Dr. Griswold, with several doctors and clergymen. As befitted such a company the phenomena were mental rather than material, but absolutely convincing. Mrs. Fox and the three daughters were the mediums. It is interesting to note that half an hour elapsed before any sounds were heard. Strong brains charged with prejudice were present and time was needed, even by those remarkable mediums, to harmonize the conditions. Then at last came slight sounds, increasing gradually in volume until they were very clear. Each member of the company in turn asked questions, some mentally, some aloud, and all attested that the correct answers were given by the knockings. The record is too long to give in detail, but some of the information was so exact and so unusual that it was absolutely convincing. It is said that nearly all the guests were converted by this remarkable experience, and that this knowledge coming when their feet were, as the future proved, on the very threshold of death, was of inestimable comfort to Cooper and to Willis.

In the presence of these extraordinary happenings it may be imagined that American science was not silent. It was loud in its mockery and disapproval. At last the flood rising from that small spring at Hydesville had become so great that it would no longer be ignored. The religious exorcisms had failed. Could not science put a stop once for all to this disturbing intrusion? There were two scientists in the United States at that time who had a European reputation. One was Agassiz, the naturalist, the other Robert Hare, the chemist, who invented among other things the oxyhydrogen blow-pipe. It was Robert Hare who went forth to slay the new delusion. He started in that thoroughly unscientific frame of mind in which science has always approached the question. He felt called upon, he said, "to bring whatever influence he possessed to the attempt to stem the tide of popular madness which, in defiance of reason and science, was fast setting in favour of the gross delusion called Spiritualism." This can hardly be called an impartial method of approaching an inquiry, and can only be compared with Faraday's contemporary assertion that in investigating such a matter one should make up one's mind beforehand what is possible and what is not. Here was a brave and honest man, however. The huge tome which recorded his investigation lies upon my table as I write. It is adorned with pictures of the spring balances, double tables, and other appliances with which he endeavoured to confound these heretics, and was himself confounded. So searching was his investigation that every source of error was eliminated. As a result Professor Hare declared after a year that he had been entirely mistaken, and that the claims of the new philosophy not only as to the phenomena, but as to their source and meaning, were absolutely justified. For this he was boycotted and bullied by the American Scientific Association, which seems to have behaved as unwisely as all of our own scientific bodies in its unreasoning opposition to what it did not comprehend. Whilst the report of this eminent scientific man was ignored, great stress was laid upon the absurd report of three unknown medical men of Buffalo, who declared that in their opinion the sounds made by the Fox sisters were caused by the repeated partial dislocations of their knee-joints. How these dislocations answered unspoken questions was not explained.

The persecution endured by Professor Hare was repeated in the case of Judge Edmonds, head of the High Court of New York, who had also approached the movement with a view to exposing it, but who found himself confounded by the appearance of phenomena within his own family circle, and by the development of his own daughter into a medium, possessing in some directions greater powers than the Fox sisters. Like Professor Hare, he proclaimed his conversion in a book, and had to leave the Bench in consequence. Such intolerance was deplorable, and yet there is this excuse for it, that numerous cranks had burst into all sorts of wild theories, and also that the vile race of spurious mediums, or of mediums who eked out real powers by faked phenomena, were beginning to appear and to cause those scandals with which we are too familiar. Unable to distinguish the true from the counterfeit, the public, busy with its own affairs and impatient with the claims of another world, was glad to dismiss the whole subject as one vast delusion.

A word must be said as to the tragic fate of the two younger Fox sisters, a subject which is painful to Spiritualists and yet must be faced. Both fell victims to that dipsomania which was hereditary in the family. Each had made a remarkably good marriage, Margaret becoming the wife of Dr. Kane, the famous Arctic explorer, while Kate married Mr. Jencken, a member of the English Bar. The latter was very thoroughly tested by Professor Crookes, who was a most severe critic of psychic powers, though opponents of the movement represent him as credulous. Margaret became a Roman Catholic, and high influences were used, according to her own account, to place her in a convent. What with religious excitement and her hereditary weakness she fell in her later years into a pitiable state, in which she alternately denounced Spiritualism, proclaiming herself an impostor, and recanted her statement with the most solemn vows. Personally, I am of opinion that she was by no means free from the suspicion that when psychic power was wanting she supplemented it by fraud. As to her final assertions and denials, I think that Father Thurston may be right when he says that both were in a sense true. Mr. Isaac Funk, the famous lexicographer, says of her in her later years, "For five dollars she would have denied her mother and sworn to anything."

I have said that such a fate befalling the early mediums is painful to their friends, but it has small bearing upon their faith. A medium is in no sense a teacher or an example, but is a passive instrument for forces outside herself. There have been, and are, many mediums who have been of saintly mould. There have been others who have yielded to some human weakness, very especially to drink. Their powers and their message are to be held distinct from themselves, as a Catholic would hold that a bad priest may celebrate a true sacrament, or a materialist that a foolish operator may transmit a wise telegram. Their weaknesses delay the acceptance of the new knowledge. It still stands upon the threshold—but the door is slowly opening.

XIV
A NEW LIGHT
ON OLD CRIMES

PSYCHIC SCIENCE, though still in its infancy, has already reached a point where we can dissect many of those occurrences which were regarded as inexplicable in past ages, and can classify and even explain them—so far as any ultimate explanation of anything is possible. So long as gravity, electricity, magnetism, and so many other great natural forces are inexplicable one must not ask too much of the youngest —though it is also the oldest—of the sciences. But the progress made has been surprising—the more surprising since it has been done by a limited circle of students whose results have hardly reached the world at large, and have been greeted rather with incredulous contempt than with the appreciation which they deserve. So far have we advanced that of the eighty or ninety cases carefully detailed in Dale Owen's *Footfalls*, published in 1859, we find now, seventy years later, that there is hardly one which cannot be classified and understood. It would be interesting, therefore, to survey some of those cases which stand on record in our law courts, and have been variously explained in the past as being either extraordinary coincidences or as interpositions of Providence. The latter phrase may well represent a fact, but people must learn that no such thing has ever been known as an interposition of Providence save through natural law, and that when it has seemed inexplicable and miraculous it is only because the law has not yet been understood. All miracles come under exact law, but the law, like all natural laws, is itself divine and miraculous.

We will endeavour in recounting these cases, which can only be done in the briefest fashion, to work from the simpler to the more complex—from that which may have depended upon the natural but undefined powers of the subconscious self, through all the range of clairvoyance and telepathy, until we come to that which seems beyond all question to be influenced by the spirit of the dead. There is one case, that of Owen Parfitt, of Shepton Mallet, in Somersetshire, which may form a starting-point, since it is really impossible to say whether it was psychic or not; but if it were not, it forms one of the most piquant mysteries which ever came before the British public.

This old fellow was a seaman, a kind of John Silver, who lived in the piratical days of the eighteenth century and finally settled down, upon what were usually considered to have been ill-gotten gains, about the year 1760, occupying a comfortable cottage on the edge of the little Somerset town. His sister kept house for him, but she was herself too infirm to look after the rheumatic old mariner, so a neighbour named Susanna Snook used to come in by the day and help to care for him. It was observed that Parfitt went periodically to Bristol, and that he returned with money, but how he gained it was his secret. He appears to have been a secretive and wicked old creature, with many strange tales of wild doings, some of which related to the West Coast of Africa, and possibly to the slave trade. Eventually his infirmity increased upon him. He could no longer get farther than his garden, and seldom left the great chair in which he was placed every day by the ministering Susanna Snook, just outside the porch of the cottage.

Then one summer morning, June 6, 1768, an extraordinary thing happened. He had been deposited as usual, with a shawl round his shoulders, while the hard-working Susanna darted back to her own cottage near-by. She was away for half an hour. When she returned she found, to her amazement, that the old seaman had disappeared. His sister was wringing her hands in great bewilderment over the shawl, which still remained upon the chair, but as to what became of the old reprobate nothing has ever been learned from that day to this. It should be emphasized that he was practically unable to walk and was far too heavy to be easily carried.

The alarm was at once given, and as the haymaking was in full swing the countryside was full of workers, who were ready to declare that even if he could have walked he could not have escaped their observation upon the roads. A search was started, but it was interrupted by a sudden and severe storm, with thunder and heavy rain. In spite of the weather, there was a general alarm for twenty-four hours, which failed to discover the least trace of the missing man. His unsavoury character, some reminiscences of the Obi men and Voodoo cult of Africa, and the sudden thunderstorm, all combined to assure the people of Somerset that the devil had laid his claws upon the old seaman; nor has any natural explanation since those days set the matter in a more normal light. There were hopes once that this had been attained when, in the year 1813, some human bones were discovered in the garden of a certain Widow Lockyer, who lived within two hundred yards of the old man's cottage. Susanna Snook was still alive, and gave evidence at the inquiry, but just as it began to appear that perhaps the old man had been coaxed away and murdered, a surgeon from Bristol shut down the whole matter by a positive declaration that the bones were those of a woman. So the affair rests till to-day.

No psychic explanation can be accepted in any case until all reasonable normal solutions have been exhausted. It is possible that those visits to Bristol were connected with blackmail, and that some deeper villain in the background found means to silence that dangerous tongue. But how was it done? It is a freakish, insoluble borderland case, and there we must leave it. The natural question arises: If you have spirit communications why are you unable to get an explanation? The answer is that spirit communication is also governed by inexorable laws, and that you might as well expect an electric current along a broken wire as to get a communication when the conditions have become impossible.

Passing on to a more definite example, let us take the case of the murder of Maria Marten, which was for a long time a favourite subject when treated at village fairs under the name of "The Mystery of the Red Barn." Maria Marten was murdered in the year 1827 by a young farmer named Corder, who should have married her but failed to do so, preferring to murder her in order to conceal the result of their illicit union. His ingenious method was to announce that he was about to marry the girl, and then at the last hour shot her dead and buried her body. He then disappeared from the neighbourhood, and gave out that he and she were secretly wedded and were living together at some unknown address.

The murder was on May 18, 1827, and for some time the plan was completely successful, the crime being more effectually concealed because Corder had left behind him instructions that the barn should be filled up with stock. The rascal sent home a few letters purporting to be from the Isle of Wight, explaining that Maria and he were living together in great contentment. Some suspicion was aroused by the fact that the postmarks of these letters were all from London, but none the less the matter might have been overlooked had it not been for the unusual action of an obscure natural law which had certainly never been allowed for in Mr. Corder's calculations.

Mrs. Marten, the girl's mother, dreamed upon three nights running that her daughter had been murdered. This in itself might count for little, since it may have only reflected her vague fears and distrust. The dreams, however, were absolutely definite. She saw in them the red barn, and even the very spot in which the remains had been deposited. The latter detail is of great importance, since it disposes of the idea that the incident could have arisen from the girl having told her mother that she had an assignation there. The dreams occurred in March, 1828, ten months after the crime, but it was the middle of April before the wife was able to persuade her husband to act upon such evidence. At last she broke down his very natural scruples, and permission was given to examine the barn, now cleared of its contents. The woman pointed to the spot and the man dug. A piece of shawl was immediately exposed, and eighteen inches below it the body itself was discovered, the horrified searcher staggering in a frenzy out of the ill-omened barn. The dress, the teeth, and some small details were enough to establish the identification.

The villain was arrested in London, where he had become, by marriage, the proprietor of a girls' school, and was engaged, at the moment of capture, in ticking off the minutes for the correct boiling of the breakfast eggs. He set up an ingenious defence, by which he tried to prove that the girl had committed suicide, but there was no doubt that it was a cold-blooded crime, for he had taken not only pistols, but also a pickaxe into the barn. This was the view which the jury took, and he was duly hanged, confessing his guilt in a half-hearted way before his execution. It is an interesting fact that the London school-mistress, whom he had trapped into marriage by means of a specious advertisement in which he described himself as a "private gentleman, whose disposition is not to be exceeded," remained devotedly attached to him to the end.

Now here is a case about which there is no possible doubt. The murder was unquestionably discovered by means of the triple dream, for which there could have been no natural explanation. There remain two psychic explanations. The one depends upon telepathy or thought-reading, a phenomenon which, of course, exists, as anyone can prove who experiments with it, but which has been stretched to most unreasonable lengths by those who would prefer any explanation to that which entails disembodied intelligence. It is, of course, within the bounds of remote possibility that the murderer thought of the girl's mother upon three successive nights and also upon the scene of the crime, thus connecting up the vision of one with the brain of the other. If any student thinks this the more probable explanation he is certainly entitled to accept it. On the other hand, there is a good deal of evidence that dreams, and especially early-in-the-morning dreams just before the final waking, do at times convey information which seems to come from other intelligences than our own. Taking all the facts, I am of opinion that the spirit of the dead woman did actually get in touch with the mind of the mother, and impressed upon her the true facts of her unhappy fate. It is to be remembered, however, that even those who advanced telepathy as an explanation of such a case are postulating a power which was utterly unknown to science until this generation, and which itself represents a great extension of our psychic knowledge. We must not allow it, however, to block our way to the further and more important advances which lie beyond it.

For purposes of comparison we will now take another dream case which is perfectly authentic. Upon February 8th, 1840, Edmund Norway, the chief officer of the ship *Orient*, at that time near St. Helena, dreamed a dream between the hours of 10 p.m. and 4 a.m. in which he saw his brother Nevell, a Cornish gentleman, murdered by two men. His brother was seen to be mounted. One of the assailants caught the horse's bridle and snapped a pistol twice, but no report was heard. He and his comrade then struck him several blows, and dragged him to the side of the road, where they left him. The road appeared to be a familiar one in Cornwall, but the house, which should have been on the right, came out upon the left in the visual picture. The dream was recorded in writing at the time, and was told to the other officers of the ship.

The murder had actually occurred, and the assassins, two brothers named Lightfoot, were executed on April 13th of that year, at Bodmin. In his confession the elder brother said: "I went to Bodmin on February 8th and met my brother . . . my brother knocked Mr. Norway down. He snapped a pistol at him twice, but it did not go off. He then knocked him down with the pistol. It was on the road to Wadebridge" (the road which had been seen in the dream). "We left the body in the water on the left side of the road coming to Wadebridge. My brother drew the body across the road to the watering." The evidence made it clear that the murder was committed between the hours of ten and eleven at night. As St. Helena is, roughly, in the same longitude as England, the time of the dream might exactly correspond with that of the crime.

These are the actual facts, and, though they may be explained, they cannot be explained away. It appears that Norway, the sailor, had been thinking of and writing to his landsman brother just before going to his bunk. This might possibly have made the subsequent vision more easy by bringing the two men into *rapport*. There is a considerable body of evidence to prove that during sleep there is some part of us, call it the etheric body, the subconscious self, or what you will, which can detach itself and visit distant scenes, though the cut-off between sleeping and waking is so complete that it is very rarely that the memory of the night's experience is carried through. I could quote many examples within my own experience of this "traveling clairvoyance," as it is called, but one which attracted a good deal of attention at the time, as it was fully described in *The Times*, was that of Sir Rider Haggard's dog, the dead body of which was found through a vision of the night. The same occurs in the stupor of high fever, and I have heard my little son, with a temperature of one hundred four degrees, make a remark in delirium which showed that he saw clearly what had occurred in the next room. "Naughty Denis, breaking my soldiers!" were the words, and they were absolutely correct. Thus it can easily be conceived that the consciousness of the sailor, drawn to his brother by recent loving thoughts, went swiftly to him in his sleep, and was so shocked to witness his murder that it was able to carry the record through into his normal memory. The case would resolve itself, then, into one which depended upon the normal but unexplored powers of the human organism, and not upon any interposition from the spirit of the murdered man. Had the vision of the latter appeared alone, without the accompanying scene, it would have seemed more probable that it was indeed a post-mortem apparition.

For the next illustration we will turn to the records of American crime. In this case, which is absolutely authentic, a man named Mortensen owed a considerable sum of money, three thousand eight hundred dollars, to a company, which was represented by the secretary, Mr. Hay. The transaction occurred in Utah in the year 1901. Mortensen beguiled Hay to his private house late in the evening, and nothing more was heard of the unfortunate man. Mortensen's story was that he paid the money in gold, and that Hay had given him a receipt and had started home with the money, carried in glass jars. When the police visited Mortensen's house in the morning they were accompanied by Hay's father-in-law, an aged Mormon named Sharp, who said: "Where did you last see my son-in-law?"

"Here," answered Mortensen, indicating a spot outside his door.

"If that is the last place you saw him," said Sharp, "then that is where you killed him."

"How do you know he is dead?" asked Mortensen.

"I have had a vision," said Sharp, "and the proof is that within one mile of the spot where you are standing, his dead body will be dug up from the field."

There was snow on the ground at the time, and next morning, December 18th, a neighbour observed some blood-stains upon it not very far from Mortensen's house. They led to a mound shaped like a grave. The neighbour procured a spade, borrowing it from Mortensen himself, and speedily unearthed the body of Hay. There was a bullet wound at the back of his head. His valuables had been untouched, but the receipt which he was known to have carried to Mortensen's house afforded sufficient reason for the murder.

The whole crime seems to have been a very crude and elementary affair, and it is difficult to see how Mortensen could have hoped to save himself, unless, indeed, an immediate flight was in his mind. There could be no adequate defence, and the man was convicted and shot—the law of Utah giving the criminal the choice as to the fashion of his own death. The only interest in the affair is the psychic one, for again old Sharp repeated at the trial that in a vision he had learned the facts. It is not a very clear case, however, and may conceivably have been a bluff upon the part of the old man, who had formed his own opinion as to the character of his son-in-law, and his probable actions. Such a solution would, however, involve a very extraordinary coincidence.

The next case which I would cite is very much more convincing—in fact, it is final in its clear proof of psychic action, though the exact degree may be open to discussion. The facts seem to have been established beyond all possible doubt, though there is some slight confusion about the date. According to the account of Mr. Williams, of Cornwall, the chief actor, it was in the early days of May, 1812, that he thrice in the same night had a remarkable dream. Mr. Williams was a man of affairs, and the superintendent of some great Cornish mines. He was familiar with the lobby of the House of Commons, into which his interests had occasionally led him. It was this lobby which he perceived clearly in his dream. His attention was arrested by a man in a snuff-coloured coat, with metal buttons, who loitered there. Presently there entered a small, brisk man in a blue coat and white waistcoat. As he passed, the first man whipped out a pistol and shot the other through the breast. In his dream Mr. Williams was made aware that the murdered man was Mr. Perceval, the Chancellor of the Exchequer. Mr. Williams was greatly impressed, and alarmed, by this dream, and he recounted it not only to his wife but also to several friends whom he met at the Godolphin mine next day, asking their advice whether he should go up to London and report the matter. To this they answered very naturally, but unfortunately as the event proved, that it was useless, and would only expose him to derision. On the thirteenth, about ten days after the dream, Mr. Williams narrates how his son, returning from Truro, rushed into the room crying, "Oh, father, your dream has come true! Mr. Perceval has been shot in the House of Commons." The deed, as is well known, was committed by a man named Bellingham, who had some imaginary grievance. The dress of the two chief actors, and all the other details, proved to be exactly as foretold.

In an account in *The Times* sixteen years later it was stated that the vision was upon the actual night of the murder, which would reduce the case to ordinary clairvoyance, but the evidence is very strong that it was prophetic as well. Mr. Williams, writing in 1832, four years after *The Times* account, repeated the story once more as it is set forth here. His wife, his friends at the mine, his projected journey to London, and his recollection of his son's arrival with the news all corroborate his version of the affair. What comment can we make upon such an incident? Explain it we cannot, but at least we can get some light upon it by examining the statements of others who have had both the clairvoyant and the prophetic faculty. One of these was Swedenborg, who exhibited it again and again, but we have no exact account from him as to how his visions came. More to the point are the notes of Mr. Turvey, of Bournemouth, a most remarkable psychic, whose *Beginnings of Seership* is one of the most illuminating books I know. Our ordinary comments must always be explanations from outside, but this gentleman, with his great powers and analytical brain, is able to give us more precious information which comes from within. Mr. Turvey was not only an extraordinary clairvoyant, capable of throwing out his own etheric body at will, and communicating at once to others the information which it brought back, but he again and again saw scenes of the future, which he put upon record and which frequently, if not invariably, were fulfilled. His description of his own sensation is very helpful and destined, I think, to be classical. He says:

"At certain times I see a sort of ribbon moving like the endless belt of a cinema film. In colour it is very pale heliotrope, and seems to vibrate very rapidly. On it are numerous little pictures, some of which appear to be engraved upon the film itself, while others are like pale-blue photographs stuck upon the film. The former refer to past, the latter to future events. The locality is judged by the scenery and climatic heat" (felt by the observer). "The dates are judged by the clearness of the pictures."

Now, applying this analysis of Mr. Turvey to the far less complete experience of Mr. Williams, we get some glimmer of light. Mr. Williams was of Welsh or Cornish stock, and predisposed to the psychic. In his busy life he could not develop it as Mr. Turvey had done, for the latter, though he was once a famous athlete, had broken in health to an extent which confined him to his chair. Yet at times his true innate powers could assert themselves, and thus he received or perceived one of those cinema visions of which Mr. Turvey speaks. Why it should have been sent him is beyond our ken. Was it to prompt him to go to London, as he so nearly did, and try to turn the stream of fate? Or was it as impersonal as were many of the prophetic visions of Mr. Turvey? One cannot say, but there is a big fact standing up as clear as the Nelson Column, and to turn away one's eyes, pretend not to see it, and make no attempt to fit it into the general scheme of the universe, is neither science nor common sense. Mr. Turvey has left it upon record that he saw more unpleasant than pleasant things, and Mr. Williams' experience was in accordance. This might be taken as supporting the idea that the visions are for the purpose of warning and prevention. When one considers that in this instance the picture of the lobby of the House of Commons was presented to one of the very few men in Cornwall who would recognize the place when they saw it, it certainly suggests that the vision did not merely happen, but came for a definite purpose. It is not to be denied that this and many other prophetic cases strengthen the argument of the fatalist, who holds that our Life's path is marked out for us. On the other hand, the student will find a certain number of cases which give a comforting assurance, that, though the general path may be indicated, there is still a certain play of events which gives room for changes in the issue. I have notes, for example, of one dream or vision in which the subject had a most clear impression of a long series of events, which ended in his going down a coal-mine, the latter experience being particularly vivid. Some months afterwards the whole long episode occurred exactly as depicted, but when they came to the coal-mine the guide said: "I had hoped to take you down the coal-mine, but it is a holiday, and the cage is not working." In another case a young officer of my acquaintance was warned by a dead comrade that they would meet again upon a certain date. The young man spent the day in his dug-out, and late in the evening was congratulating himself upon having got through, when about 10 p.m. his Company Commander came round and said: "I fear I must ask you to do a rather dirty job. We have to find if there are any of our dead near the German wire. Take a few men and make an examination." He gave himself up as lost, and his batman, who had heard the story, burst into tears. The young fellow was so convinced of his own impending fate that he left his party safe in No Man's Land, thinking that there was no use in their being sacrificed also. He went forward alone, made a perfectly successful search, returned in safety, and had no misfortune at all. Such a case must hearten up those who are overburdened by any prophecy or presentiment. It may be that some force—prayer, perhaps—can divert the stream of fate.

We shall now turn to some cases which were more clearly ultramundane in their nature, and I would express my obligation to Mr. Harold Furniss, whose care has restored many details in his collection of criminal records. The first which I would choose is the murder of Sergeant Davies in the Highlands in the year 1749. Davies was part of the English garrison left in the north after the suppression of Prince Charlie's rising, and, like many of his comrades, he alleviated his exile by the excellent sport which the barren country afforded. Upon September 28th in that year he went shooting near Braemar without any attendant. The rancour of the recent war had to some extent died down, and in any case the sergeant, who was a powerful and determined man, feared no opponent. The result showed, however, that he was overbold, as he never returned from his expedition. Search parties were sent out, but months passed and there were still no signs of the missing soldier. Five years passed, and the mystery was still unsolved. At the end of that time, two Highlanders, Duncan Terig and Alex. Bain Macdonald, were arrested because the fowling-piece and some of the property of the lost man were found in their possession. The case rested mainly, however, upon some evidence which was as strange as any ever heard in a court of law.

A farm labourer named Alex. Macpherson, aged twenty-six, deposed that one night in the summer of 1750—that is, some nine months after the sergeant's disappearance—he was lying awake in the barn where all the servants slept, when he saw enter a man dressed in blue, who came to his bedside and beckoned him to follow. Outside the door the figure turned and said: "I am Sergeant Davies." The apparition then pointed to a distant moss or swamp, and said: "You will find my bones there. Go and bury them at once, for I can have no peace, nor will I give you any, until my bones are buried, and you may get Donald Farquharson to help you." It then vanished.

Early next day Macpherson, according to his own account, went to the place indicated and, obeying the exact instructions received, he came straight upon the body, still wearing the blue regimental coat of Guise's Horse. Macpherson laid it upon the surface, dragging it out from the slime, but did not bury it. A few nights later the vision appeared to him once more as he lay in the barn, and reproached him with having failed to carry out the instructions given. Macpherson asked: "Who murdered you?" To this the apparition answered: "Duncan Terig and Alex. Macdonald," and vanished once more. Macpherson next day went to Farquharson and asked him to come and help bury the body, to which the latter agreed. It was accordingly done. No one else was told of the incident save only one friend, John Grewar, who was informed within two days of the burial.

This story was certainly open to criticism, as the arrest was in 1754, and the alleged apparition and subsequent burial in 1750, so that one would naturally ask why no information had been given during four years. On the other hand, one could imagine that these Celtic Highlanders were somewhat in the position of Irish peasants in an agrarian outrage. They were bound together against a common enemy, and would not act save under pressure. This pressure arrived when the two suspects were actually arrested, the murdered man's gear was found upon them, and direct inquiry was made from the folk in the neighbourhood. No ill-will was shown to exist between Macpherson and the accused men, nor was any motive alleged for so extraordinary a concoction. On the psychic side there are also some objections. One would have conceived that the sergeant might return, as others seem to have done, in order to identify his murderers, but in this case that was a secondary result, and the main one appears to have been the burial of his own remains. Spirits are not much concerned about their own bodies. In a communication which I saw recently, the deceased alluded to his body as "that thing that I used to go about in." Still, earthly prejudices die hard, and if Davies, sprung from a decent stock, yearned for a decent burial, it would surely not be an unnatural thing.

There was some corroboration for Macpherson's weird story. There were female quarters in this barn, and a woman worker, named Isabel Machardie, deposed that on the second occasion of the apparition she saw "something naked come in at the door and go straight to Macpherson's bed, which frightened her so much that she drew the clothes over her head." She added that when it appeared it came in a bowing posture, but she could not tell what it was. The next morning she asked Macpherson what it was that had troubled them the night before, and he answered that she might be easy, for it would trouble them no more.

There is a discrepancy here between the blue-coated figure of the first vision, and the "something naked" of the second, but the fact remained that the woman claimed to have seen something alarming, and to have alluded to it next day. Macpherson, however, could speak nothing but Gaelic, his evidence being interpreted to the Court. Lockhart, the defending barrister, naturally asked in what tongue the vision spoke, to which Macpherson answered: "In as good Gaelic as ever I heard in Lochaber." "Pretty good for the ghost of an English sergeant," said Lockhart, and this facile retort made the Court laugh, and finally brought about the acquittal of the prisoners, in spite of the more material proofs which could not be explained away. Later, both Lockhart and the advocate engaged with him, admitted their belief in the guilt of their clients.

As a matter of fact, Davies had fought at Culloden in April, 1746, and met his end in September, 1749, so that he had been nearly three and a half years in the Highlands, mixing in sport with the gillies, and it is difficult to suppose that he could not muster a few simple sentences of their language.

But apart from that, although our information shows that knowledge has to be acquired by personal effort, and not by miracle, in the after life, still it is to be so acquired, and if Sergeant Davies saw that it was only in a Gael that he would find those rare psychic gifts which would enable him to appear and to communicate (for every spirit manifestation must have a material basis), then it is not inconceivable that he would master the means during the ten months or so which elapsed before his reappearance. Presuming that Macpherson's story is true, it by no means follows that he was the medium, since any one of the sleepers in the barn might have furnished that nameless atmosphere which provides the correct conditions. In all such cases it is to be remembered that this atmosphere is rare, and that a spirit comes back not as it would or when it would, but as it can. Law, inexorable law, still governs every fresh annexe which we add to our knowledge, and only by defining and recognizing its limitations will we gain some dim perception of the conditions of the further life and its relation to the present one.

We now pass to a case where the spirit interposition seems to have been as clearly proved as anything could be. It was, it is true, some time ago, but full records are still available. In the year 1632 a yeoman named John Walker lived at the village of Great Lumley, some miles north of Durham. A cousin named Anne Walker kept house for him, and intimacy ensued, with the prospect of the usual results. John Walker greatly feared the scandal, and took diabolical steps to prevent it. He sent the young woman over to the town of Chester-le-Street to the care of one Dame Carr. To this matron Anne Walker confessed everything, adding that Walker had used the ominous phrase "that he would take care both of her and of her child." One night at Dame Carr's door there appeared the sinister visage of Mark Sharp, a Blackburn collier, with a specious message which induced the girl to go with him into the dusk. She was never seen again. Walker, upon being appealed to by Dame Carr, said that it was all right, and that it was better in her condition that she should be among strangers. The old lady had her suspicions, but nothing could be done, and the days passed on.

A fortnight later a miller, named James Graham, was grinding corn in his mill at night some miles away. It was after midnight when he descended to the floor of the mill after putting a fresh fill of corn in the hopper. His exact experience, as preserved in the Bodleian Library at Oxford, was as follows:

"The mill door being shut, there stood a woman in the midst of the floor, with her hair hanging down all bloody, with five large wounds on her head. He being much amazed began to bless himself, and at last asked her who she was and what she wanted. She answered, 'I am the spirit of Anne Walker, who lived with John Walker. . . . He promised to send me to where I should be well looked to . . . and then I should come again and keep his house. I was one night sent away with Mark Sharp, who, upon a certain moor' (naming the place) 'slew me with a pick such as men dig coal with and gave me these five wounds, and after threw my body into a coalpit hard by, and hid the pick under a bank, and his shoes and stockings being bloody he endeavoured to wash them, but seeing the blood would not part he hid them there.'"

The spirit ended by ordering the miller to reveal the truth on pain of being haunted.

In this case, as in the last, the message was not delivered. The horrified miller was so impressed that he would by no means be alone, but he shirked the delicate task which had been confided to him. In spite of all his precautions, however, he found himself alone one evening, with the result that the vision instantly reappeared, "very fierce and cruel," to use his description, and insisted that he should do as commanded. More obdurate than the Celtic Macpherson, the miller awaited a third summons, which came in so terrific a form in his own garden that his resistance was completely broken down, and so, four days before Christmas, he went to the nearest magistrate and lodged his deposition. Search was at once made, and the vision was justified in all particulars, which, it must be admitted, has not always been the case where information has seemed to come from beyond. The girl's body, the five wounds in the head, the pick, the bloodstained shoes and stockings were all found, and as the body was in a deep coal-pit there seemed no normal means by which the miller could possibly have known the nature of the wounds unless he had himself inflicted them, which is hardly consistent either with the known facts, with his appearance as informer, or with the girl's admissions to Dame Carr.

John Walker and Mark Sharp were both arrested and were tried for murder at the Durham Assizes before Judge Davenport. It was shown that the miller was unknown, save by sight, to either prisoner, so that it could not be suggested that he had any personal reason for swearing away their lives by a concocted tale. The trial was an extraordinary one, for there seems to have been a psychic atmosphere such as has never been recorded in a prosaic British court of law. The foreman of the jury, a Mr. Fairbairn, declared in an affidavit that he saw during the trial the "likeness of a child standing upon Walker's shoulder." This might be discounted as being the effect upon an emotional nature of the weird evidence to which he had listened, but it received a singular corroboration from the judge, who wrote afterwards to a fellow-lawyer, Mr. Serjeant Hutton, of Goldsborough, that he himself was aware of a figure such as Fairbairn described, and that during the whole proceedings he was aware of a most uncanny and unusual sensation for which he could by no means account. The verdict was guilty, and the two men were duly executed.

The array of responsible witnesses in this case was remarkable. There was the judge himself, Mr. Fairbairn, with his affidavit, Mr. James Smart, Mr. William Lumley, of Great Lumley, and others. Altogether, it is difficult to see how any case could be better authenticated, and I have no doubt myself that the facts were as stated, and that this single case is enough to convince an unprejudiced mind of the continuance of individuality and of the penetrability of that screen which separates us from the dead.

What comment can psychic science make upon such an episode? In the first place, I would judge that the miller was a powerful medium—that is, he exuded that rare atmosphere which enables a spirit to become visible as the meteorite becomes visible when it passes through the atmosphere of earth. It is, I repeat, a rare quality, and in this case seems to have been unknown to its possessor, though I should expect to find that the miller had many other psychic experiences which took a less public form. This is the reason why the apparition did not appear before the magistrate himself, but could only approach him by messenger. The spirit may have searched some time before she found her medium, just as Sergeant Davies was ten months before he found the Highlander who had those physical qualities which enabled him to communicate. Law and obedience to law run through the whole subject. It is also abundantly evident that the confiding woman who had been treated with such cold-blooded ingratitude and treachery carried over to the other world her natural feelings of indignation and her desire for justice. As a curious detail it is also evident that she recovered her consciousness instantly after death, and was enabled to observe the movements of her assassin. With what organs, one may ask? With what organs do we see clear details in a dream? There is something there besides our material eyes.

A most reasonable objection may be urged as to why many innocent people have suffered death and yet have experienced no super-normal help which might have saved them. Any criminologist could name offhand a dozen cases where innocent men have gone to the scaffold. Why were they not saved? I have written in vain if I have not by now enabled the reader to answer the question himself. If the physical means are not there, then it is impossible. It may seem unjust, but not more so than the fact that a ship provided with wireless may save its passengers while another is heard of no more. The problem of unmerited suffering is part of that larger problem of the functions of pain and evil, which can only be explained on the supposition that spiritual chastening and elevation come in this fashion, and that this end is so important that the means are trivial in comparison. We must accept this provisional explanation, or we are faced with chaos.

Can these dim forces which we see looming above and around us be turned to the use of man? It would be a degradation to use them for purely material ends, and it would, in my opinion, bring some retribution with it; but, where the interests of Justice are concerned, I am convinced that they could indeed be used to good effect. Here is a case in point.

Two brothers, Eugene and Paul Dupont, lived some fifty years ago in the Rue St. Honoré of Paris. Eugene was a banker, Paul a man of letters. Eugene disappeared. Every conceivable effort was made to trace him, but the police finally gave it up as hopeless. Paul was persevering, however, and in company with a friend, Laporte, he visited Mme. Huerta, a well-known clairvoyante, and asked for her assistance.

We have no record as to how far articles of the missing man were given to the medium, as a bloodhound was started on a trail, but whether it was by psychometry or not, Mme. Huerta, in the mesmerized state, very quickly got in touch with the past of the two brothers, from the dinner where they had last met. She described Eugene, and followed his movements from the hour that he left the restaurant until he vanished into a house which was identified without difficulty by her audience, though she was unable to give the name of the street. She then described how inside the house Eugene Dupont had held a conference with two men whom she described, how he had signed some paper and had received a bundle of bank notes. She then saw him leave the house, she saw the two men follow him, she saw two other men join in the pursuit, and finally she saw the four assault the banker, murder him, and throw the body into the Seine.

Paul was convinced by the narrative, but his comrade, Laporte, regarded it as a fabrication. They had no sooner reached home, however, than they learned that the missing man had been picked out of the river and was exposed at the Morgue. The police, however, were inclined to take the view of suicide, as a good deal of money was in the pockets. Paul Dupont knew better, however. He hunted out the house, he discovered that the occupants did business with his brother's firm, he found that they held a receipt for two thousand pounds in exchange for notes paid to his brother on the night of the crime, and yet those notes were missing. A letter making an appointment was also discovered.

The two men, a father and son, named Dubuchet, were then arrested, and the missing links were at once discovered. The pocketbook which Eugene Dupont had in his possession on the night of the murder was found in Dubuchet's bureau. Other evidence was forthcoming, and finally the two villains were found guilty and were condemned to penal servitude for life. The medium was not summoned as a witness, on the ground that she was not conscious at the time of her vision, but her revelations undoubtedly brought about the discovery of the crime.

Now it is clear in this authentic case that the police would have saved themselves much trouble, and come to a swifter conclusion, had they themselves consulted Mme. Huerta in the first instance. And if it is obviously true in this case, why might it not be so in many other cases? It should be possible at every great police-centre to have the call upon the best clairvoyant or other medium that can be got, and to use them freely, for what they are worth. None are infallible. They have their off-days and their failures. No man should ever be convicted upon their evidence. But when it comes to suggesting clues and links, then it might be invaluable. In the case of Mr. Foxwell, the London stock-broker who fell into the Thames some years ago, it is well known that the mode of his death, and the place where his body would be found, were described by Von Bourg, the crystal-gazer, and that it was even as he had said. I venture to say that the mere knowledge that the police had an ally against whom every cunning precaution might prove unavailing would in itself be a strong deterrent to premeditated crime. This is so obvious, that if it had not been for vague scientific and religious prejudices, it would surely have been done long ago. Its adoption may be one of the first practical and material benefits given by psychic science to humanity.

XV

SINGULAR RECORDS
OF A CIRCLE

I HAVE recently received a considerable bundle of records from a circle sitting in Uruguay. The sitters consisted of two Englishmen of the best class, whom I will call "Hudson." They have given me permission to use their real names, but perhaps they hardly realize how considerable the backwash might be from such a publication. A lady friend, Miss Reader, is the medium, and the procedure is by means of a glass and the alphabet in the usual fashion.

The number of real or alleged spirits that came to this circle and their communications have been so clear and direct and present such extraordinary variety that they invite comment. After reading their record, which has been very well taken, I guarded myself by getting each member of the circle to sign a document putting them upon their word of honour that no hoax was intended. The elder Mr. Hudson adds: "The way in which spirits of different character came through, one after the other, and the unexpectedness and spontaneity of the answers with the different styles and phrases would have taxed better imaginations than those possessed by any of the three of us."

I particularly inquired whether they had any special acquaintance with the English public schools and whether they had done any particular reading as to seventeenth- or eighteenth-century life. The answer to the first question was that they had both been Eton boys, but that they knew nothing of any other school, and the answer to the second was that none of them had any particular knowledge of the centuries named.

When I say that among the visitants were two very exuberant public-school boys, four ladies of easy virtue, one old sea captain, one Austrian adventurer who had been murdered, and a number of bucks from the Regency and earlier years, it will be realized that the communications really seemed of unusual nature. They were full of points which might be evidential and I have taken some trouble to follow these up, sometimes with striking success and sometimes with complete failure.

The first visitant who came on December 18th, 1928, and on several subsequent occasions, was one Nicholas, who refused to give his surname. He said he had just died, having been shot in Vienna. He was forty-one years of age, had lived an evil life and was intensely unhappy in the other world. He was born in Baku, had gone to Germany afterwards, as an Austrian he had served in the war, against the Russians, had been taken prisoner and sent to Siberia, had been liberated by the Communists, but had been arrested by the Bolshevists as a spy, not making his escape until 1926. Then he went to Vienna, where he had an intrigue with an English girl who had gone there to study art. In the course of this intrigue he had been shot, presumably by some jealous rival. The story seems to me to hang together fairly well, though there is no means of verifying the statements. It is worth noting that the sitters had some little difficulty as to where Baku might be, and were corrected at once by the visitor.

The next comer was an exceedingly flighty youth who gave the name of Lionel Vereker, but admitted that the surname had not been disclosed. He was a practical joker, and his answers to questions are so full of levity, sometimes witty and sometimes foolish, that it is difficult to know when one is to take him seriously. When his jokes were not appreciated he seems to have got sulky. When pressed to his surname he said, "I think, in the excitement of dying, I forgot it." In his more sober moments he said that he had been educated at Dulwich and that he left school in the year 1920. When asked what house he was at there, he replied, "Alleyne's." I find on inquiring, that "Alleyne" was actually the founder of Dulwich College, so that this reply was evidential if we accept the assurance of the sitters that they had no knowledge of the matter, which I may say I unreservedly do. Judging by his high spirits he seems perfectly happy. He gave the impression of being an irresponsible fribble with no great harm in him and no great good. I can well believe that there are impersonations at séances if Lionel was around. I inquired at Dulwich, but the name could not be traced.

The next visitor, December 29th, 1928, was a very interesting personage. This was Harriette Wilson, the famous courtesan of the beginning of last century, who numbered among her lovers both the Duke of Wellington and the Duke of Argyll. She wrote a volume of Memoirs which show that in spite of her profession she was in many ways a woman of fine character. The circle seems to have known that such a person existed and also that she wrote Memoirs, so to that extent the evidence is weakened. She gives, however, some details which have been found on examination to be approximately correct and which could hardly have been known by them. She says, for example, that she died a hundred years ago. She actually left London in 1826, lived in Paris for a short time and then seems to have disappeared. I have often wondered whether she had been poisoned. She had promised to write a second book of "Memoirs," mentioning the names of quite a string of people whom she would inculpate. The spirit says she was thirty-nine when she died. She was, I think thirty-six when she left London. The monologue with her concludes thus:

Q. "Are you happy?"—A. "No."

Q. "Have you others to whom you can talk?"—A. "Yes" (glass moves violently).

Q. "Don't you like them?"—A. "No" (furiously).

Q. "Why?"—A. "I don't find them to my taste."

Q. "Do you know us?"—A. "No, who are you? Interesting?"

Q. "Have you talked to others on this earth?"—A. "Yes. Many."

Q. "Can you materialise?"—A. "No, I wish I could."

Q. "Have you got any particular message?"—A. "No."

So appeared Harriette after a hundred years. She does not seem to have found the peace which some of her kindly actions upon earth deserved.

The message seems to be evidential unless I could suppose that members of the circle in Uruguay had hunted up details which I have had some difficulty in getting in London.

The next visitor was one Catherine Wimpole, who claimed that she had died at the age of twelve, one hundred and sixteen years before—or in 1812. She had lived in Clarges Street. It is remarkable that in nearly every case the communicator, readily and without hesitation gave the names of streets which did exist at that time, and never made any mistake as to the monarch who reigned then. There was nothing of a really evidential character from Catherine Wimpole, and a Spiritualist must feel surprise that one who died as an innocent girl of twelve so long ago had not progressed beyond the somewhat mediocre crowd who assembled round this circle.

The next was a James Kirk, who claimed to have been a gentleman who died of an unknown pest in the year 1749 in London. It would be interesting to know if the City had any such visitation in that year. When asked who was King he at once replied, "George the Second." He said that he lived in a grey twilight and was not happy, having none of the luxury to which he was used. It was his first return to earth and it gave him pleasure. He said that he had been in several spheres, and he asked what London was like now. He said that he had been a theatre-goer, that his favourite actress was Mrs. Oldfield and that he had liked her best in "The Country Wife." He died in Duke Street, which is or was out of the Strand. He went often to Court. He named Louis Quatorze as King of France, which of course would not be correct at the time of Kirk's death, but that great monarch would have filled the years of his youth and have left the strongest impression upon his mind, so that the error should not be judged too harshly. He was then asked for a statement as to his own life and he wrote as follows:

"I had a full life. More than my share of entertainment; balls, theatres, and such diversions. I became enamoured many times to no purpose. I was too much like the famous Captain Macheath. (We exclaim at this.) So you also know? I was a friend of the Lady Mary Montague. Perhaps you have not heard her name? (No.) She was a beautiful woman, brilliant in her own circle. I saw the execution of the notorious Jack Sheppard on Tyburn Hill. Did you ever hear of Mrs. Cornelys? (No.) She was the owner of a kind of public ball-room or rooms. She and her daughter became involved in difficulties and eventually disappeared from London, which caused endless idle speculation and gossip. I fought two duels; was, I fear, wounded fatally in the second; but as you perceive, I did not fare too bad. I frequently travelled to Harrogate, Tonbridge and Bath; generally I confess, in quest of the newest aspirant to my name. I enjoyed existence; there was much to occupy one's mind. I was fond, inordinately fond, of dress. Most of every pleasure I doted upon the theater. I went without fail to the new plays presented."

Now this reads extraordinarily true. The "Beggar's Opera" was all the vogue at the time and Captain Macheath would be a most natural allusion. Mary Montague was, of course, as stated and comes within the dates. Jack Sheppard was executed at Tyburn in 1724. Finally, Madame Cornelys is excellent. How many are there who have heard of her? By a chance note in an old book I found that she was the proprietor at that time of a very popular dancing-place at the corner of Soho Square, and that she went bankrupt. I think that this sequence of correct references is beyond all guess or coincidence and that we may take James Kirk at his face value.

He was fifty-three when he died, so that he was born in 1698. When asked if he would come again he replied that he would be "full glad." His health, he said, was excellent. "The Cocoa Tree" was his favourite resort upon earth, and Mr. Oliver Penberthy of St. James' his best friend. He was at his best among the fair sex.

The next actor upon this curious stage was one David Overman who claimed to be an Uppingham boy, but whose name is not upon the school lists. There is a mystery in names and possibly some prohibition upon their use in a way which would hurt surviving relations. The evidence of the last comer shows that even when the name of the communicator may be wrong his allusions are quite correct. David Overman was an irresponsible person, very much like Lionel Vereker, for whom he professed great contempt. "A perfect fool" was his description. Overman left school, according to his account, in 1917, did not go to the war, and died at the age of twenty-seven. He seems to have been in a cheerful, frivolous sphere. The dialogue runs:

Q. "Where is Lionel?"—A. "Off on the gay, I expect."
Q. "Any ladies there?"—A. "Plenty. Too many."
Q. "Are you restricted?"—A. "Not unreasonably. We can even dance."
Q. "What clothes?"—A. "Any. I wear a very handsome suit of plus-fours."
Q. "Did you die in them?"—A. "Yes."
Q. "Of what?"—A. "Motor accident. Nasty man. Quick car."

Q. "Instantly killed?"—A. "Yes."

Q. "Where?"—A. "On the Portsmouth Road between Esher and Kingston."

It would be interesting to know whether in 1927 or 1928 a youth of twenty-seven answering to this description was killed in the manner indicated. His only other information was that he was attached to "a very natty young woman," Betty Matthews, on his side of life. Also that he did not go to the University. There is nothing evidential in all this, but the details are plausible and possibly some of them may be corroborated.

The next visitant was Edward Keith of Lincoln, who died in 1870 of small-pox, being sixty-four years of age. He said that he found difficulty in communicating and he soon stopped. There was no means of checking this witness.

We now come to a very gay young lady with the curious name of Norah Sallast. Norah died at the age of nineteen, seventy-eight years ago, which takes her back to the middle of the last century.

Q. "Are you happy?"—A. "No."

Q. "Why?"—A. "Life is so monotonous. I hate it" (violently).

Q. "Is it dark?"—A. "No, light."

Q. "Have you anyone to talk to?"—A. "Yes. I hate it all. You can do little to help me. I was wrong in my life."

Q. "And you suffer for it?"—A. "Quite enough."

Q. "Any prospect of happiness?"—A. "I doubt it."

Q. "In what way were you wrong?"—A. "Bad (violently). Rotten all through. I could not be thought immoral, as I knew not the meaning of the word."

She then proceeded to give a sketch of her life which was certainly rather hectic considering that she died at nineteen. She ran away from school with a mysterious man. "He gave me a hell upon earth. I left him and life was a series of meetings and separations—Budapest, Berlin, everywhere—I had no money of my own. I was stranded in Sicily and found my way home. I lived in London for five years. I was only thirteen when I ran from school. I spent two days in Bristol and died there."

This pitiable story hangs together and yet is incapable of proof. Taking it as true it seems a long purgatory for so young a sinner. One could imagine that she, like Harriette Wilson, is held until she has realized that the seeking of excitement is not the object of life. Had the sitters been experienced Spiritualists this would, of course, have been pointed out to her, and a new era have, perhaps, been started.

The next comer was curious, though hard to verify. The name given was Niel Hamilton. He was twelve years old when he was drowned at Cuckfield in Sussex, more than a century ago. He had been pushed into a duck pond, when playing. He said that he was happy, but he gave no reason why he had not progressed further in so long a time.

We now make a big leap backwards and come upon Charles Amor, who died in 1658, at the age of eighty-one. He had lived at Fleet in Hampshire. When asked who was King, he answered promptly, "No one. Cromwell." Which, of course, is correct but might have stumped some of us. He had gone to Germany, his wife had eloped with a German and he had stabbed the man. Possibly this hasty temper may have kept him so long in the purgatorial regions. There was nothing really evidential.

The next comer took us further back still. His name was John Castle, who died in 1613, at the age of ninety-two. He gave James as the name of the King, at which the circle remonstrated, but John Castle proved to be correct. This seems an important evidential point, for please do not forget that I have the signed word of honour of all concerned that there was no deception. I have always found that a British word of honour is worth more than an oath. He was a learned man, but was asked frivolous questions by the circle, who certainly played down to their visitors and had no idea of the limits of spirit power.

The next was so definite that I had high hopes, but, alas, they came to nothing. The name was Laura Yelverton. She died early in 1928 at Torquay. The Register, however, in that town failed to trace her. She was thirty-one at the time of her death. She claimed that she was born at Chester, went to school in Switzerland, lived for years at Arcachon in the South of France, lost money, returned to England in 1918, was a married woman. In reference to her surroundings she said that "it is all grey and almost sticky in the atmosphere." There were many to whom to talk. She, like the last, seems to be in some sort of purgatory. Possibly this account may meet the eye of someone who can corroborate. A note to Crowborough would always find me.

She was immediately succeeded by a man, Mark Lamb, who died in 1725. He, at once, said that George the First was on the throne, which is, of course, correct but might not be answered by everyone. He was seventy-eight when he died and he put his death to excess in living. He lived in Charles Street, London, and was a man of fashion, going to Court. He disliked the King. "His character I hated vastly." So I should think—the coarse little boor. Here we have nothing evidential but everything plausible.

He was at once succeeded by Peter Lamb, a carpenter, who died of a poisoned arm at Chatham at the age of fifty in the year 1924. He had nothing to say save that he was unfit to go to the war.

The next spirit seems to have been more intelligent and of a higher grade than any of the others. He gave some prophecies which seem to have been fairly accurate. Then comes the following:

Q. "Is it pleasant where you are?"—A. "Very. I am happy. I have interesting companionship."

Q. "Do you hope to rise higher?"—A. "I do earnestly."

Q. "Is there reincarnation?"—A. "Yes" (violently).

Q. "Have you risen higher since you died?"—A. "Yes, twice."

This is the kind of vital information which we want. As to reincarnation, it is clear at any rate that it is at only long intervals, since in three centuries he had not himself experienced it.

The next visitor gave the name of John. He was a half Spaniard who interlarded his remarks with Spanish words which were, of course, intelligible to the audience. He had been killed some fifty years ago, that would mean about 1879, on some steps in Madrid. It was in a fight with a rival over a woman. He was very unhappy, "I hate my surroundings." He was English on his mother's side. Nothing could be done to help him. His case seemed to be a bad one. There was nothing evidential.

There followed a very sprightly young lady named Willette, who claimed to be the girl of that "will of the wisp" Lionel Vereker. She did not like proper people. "Life is quite good here." She had died in 1928 in England. "What a hole!" she added. She came from Dresden, had red hair and was fond of laughing. She had talked to other people at séances, mentioning two names, Kenneth Gardner and Ruth Cameron. She was bored with Lionel—a cheerful irresponsible person—non-evidential.

The next called himself Peter Morrison, almost certainly using a false name if he exists at all. He had died in 1924 in Birmingham, aged forty-one. He had been in the war as a Lieut.-Commander in the R.N.V.R. He was on the *Warspite*. Educated at Bradfield, born in Nottingham.

This was very disappointing, as inquiry both at Bradfield and at the Admiralty failed to find any Peter Morrison. Always we seemed to break down upon the individual name even when other names were convincingly correct.

It is noticeable how often they use Christian names only, as if they did not desire identification. Thus the next called himself "Robin." He had been over two hundred years "a gentleman of much leisure and pleasure. I lived in London and Worcester." Asked if he knew James Kirk, who seemed a kindred soul, he answered, "No, is he a well-known man?" Robin soon departed. The next was also very short. Rose Lonsdale was the name. She had died in early Victorian days, aged sixty-four. Her life was uninteresting. She was always tired. She could speak a little German because she had a German music master. Nothing evidential or instructive.

The next gave the name of James Welby and he made the comprehensive remark, "we live as mortals do." He had died two centuries before at the age of fifty-two. Died from a severe cold. When asked who was king he said that George the First was on the throne. George I died in 1727, so that would be fairly correct. He lived at Salisbury and was a man of leisure. He was born in Hampshire. His parents bought him a large house in London or he added, "on the outskirts of that noble city. It was just outside of Piccadilly." Afterwards he travelled in France and married an Irish lady, named Cecilia Abby. When asked the name of his London home he replied, "It had simply the name of Dunton House." This place I have been unable to identify. He continued, "We went to all entertainments, routs and such frivolous amusements. We were blessed with two daughters, one alas, died of small-pox. The other married George Fountain. My wife died and I then lived in Salisbury, contracted a severe chill and died." The dialogue then ran:

Q. "Are you happy?"—A. "Extremely."

Q. "Are your wife and daughter with you?"—A. "Yes."

Q. "And your other daughter?"—A. "I wish I knew." (This is interesting.)

He was then asked if he knew Robin and he answered he knew

Robert Castle who often called himself Robin. They suggested that Robin lived in London and Worcester, and he replied, "No, this one lived in Cheshire." He then added that he was happy and that his surroundings were more or less like the earth he knew, but more happy and less troubled.

There is nothing evidential here, but it is very reassuring to us mortals who follow on the trail.

We now come on Richard Merriman who died in 1560 and is, therefore, the oldest spirit of all. Asked who was king at that time, he replied instantly, "Queen." "Which one?" they asked. "What other, but our Elizabeth?" He died at sea at the age of thirty-five. He caught "the feared disease. Was not able to obtain help of any competence. We had no surgeon aboard." Nothing further of importance was gathered.

Then came Katie, who refused to give a second name. She died in 1764. When asked who was king, she replied, "George the Second while I lived." This was quite correct, as George the Third came on in 1760.

The accuracy of these historical dates is really a strong point for the proof of the reality of these visitors.

Q. "How old were you?"—A. "Thirty. A great age for a woman of my kind."

Q. "Were you a woman of easy virtue?"—A. "If you care to word it thus."

Q. "Could you tell us the names of some of your lovers."—A. "Arthur Grenville, Will Roberts, Laurence Annaly. There are none worth my attention."

The conversation abruptly broke off. The next witness gave me more trouble than any of the others and some disappointment, since I seemed to be continually on the edge of what would be evidential and yet never could attain it. I was greatly helped by the courtesy of the Secretary of Lloyds' Shipping Register. The name given was John Coke. He said that he was a sailor and had been drowned eighty years ago in a shipwreck off the Virgin Islands. He asked them to pronounce his name as Cook. When asked if he was happy he said, "Not very. I miss the sea. It meant a lot to a man like me." Asked if any of his old shipmates were with him, he said, "Yes, two, but not my friends." "It is very black," he added. "I like light, I like wind and sea and salt and sun and sails. I think you do not have many sails now." Buenos Aires was a bleak town in his time. He seemed surprised to learn that it was now a great city. He was English by birth. Born at a village, Bolderstone in Norfolk. (The nearest I could get to that, after long inquiry, was Blunderstone.) He was a mate. His ship sailed from Hull to the West Indies. They were carrying back a cargo of sugar and fruit. The name of the captain was "Molleson." The name of the ship, *The Mary of Kintyre*, about two thousand tons. He was forty and unmarried.

By search we found that there was a vessel, *The Marion Macintyre*, but the name "Molleson" was not connected with it. There was, however, a vessel named *Mary* with "Morrison" as the master's name, in 1846. Her subsequent movements could not be traced. The tonnage seemed to be excessive for those days. It has been suggested that "Gorleston" which is a seaside village from which a sailor might well originate, is the right name and Bolderstone a mistake. This, however, seems a little far-fetched. On the whole we must admit that my search has not been successful in identifying John Coke.

Only one other case remains to be examined. It was that of Zoe, a lady of light virtue who claims to have met her death two years ago at Tours. She was stabbed or shot by her lover. I made some inquiries from a friend at Tours, but here again I was unable to verify the facts. Zoe, judging by her dialogue, was an amusing and rather impertinent person. Her remarks took the form of rather broad chaff of the people in the circle. Once again we have to admit there is nothing evidential.

One very curious thing about this series of cases is the number of them who died by violence. Zoe was murdered, John was murdered, Nicholas was executed, Overman died in a motor smash, Coke was drowned. The death of Harriette Wilson, is in my opinion, extremely doubtful. Therefore quite a large proportion of the cases came to their end in an untimely way. Whether this determined their presence in the particular stratum which this circle seems to have tapped is more than we can say. Apparently it was not one stratum alone, since about half of the communicants said that they were happy and the other half miserable, half being in light and the other half in gloom. Though, of course, in this world we do find happy and unhappy people living in close proximity.

I give the facts as reported and I give my analysis as far as I have been able to make it, and while there is much which is unsatisfactory, there is a great deal which is plausible and which was entirely outside the knowledge of the circle. It is just possible that this publication may bring some fresh evidence on one point or another, and such evidence would be very welcome to me. When compared with other such records there is enough in common to give us good reason to believe that we are, in some sort of dim fashion, gaining an actual glimpse of the conditions of life in a certain section of the purgatorial world.